Product Owner and User Story Training

Part of the Agile Education Series™

Copyright Notice 2019.

▸ Unless otherwise noted, these materials and the presentation of them are based on the methodology developed by Cape Project Management, Inc. and are copyrighted materials of Cape Project Management, Inc., which are used with its permission. Cape Project Management, Inc. reserves all its rights.

▸ All other brand or product names used in this guide are trade names or registered trademarks of their respective owners.

▸ PSPO I and PSMI I is a trademark of Scrum.org

▸ Portions of this slide deck are attributable to Mountain Goat Software, LLC under Creative Commons.

▸ The "Sprint Game" is adapted from the XP Game under Creative Commons:

Version 3.0

Agile Ice Breaker

The
Marshmallow Challenge

20 sticks of spaghetti + one yard tape + one yard string + one marshmallow

3

CAPE PROJECT
MANAGEMENT, INC.

Introductions and Expectations

4

 CAPE PROJECT
MANAGEMENT, INC.

About Us

- The course curriculum developed by Dan Tousignant, PMI-ACP, CSP of Cape Project Management, Inc.
- We provide public, onsite and online training:
  ○ AgileProjectManagementTraining.com
- Follow us on Twitter @ScrumDan

- The content of this course is licensed to your instructor.

5   Copyrighted material. 2019

The Agile Education Series™

1. Scrum Master Certification Training
2. Product Owner and User Story Training
3. All About Agile™: PMI-ACP® Agile Exam Preparation
4. Kanban for Software Development Teams
5. Achieving Agility – How to implement Agile in your organization
6. Agile for Team Members
7. Agile for Executives
8. Agile Testing Strategies

- All of these curriculums are available on Amazon at:
  ○ http://bit.ly/DansAgileBooks

6   Copyrighted material. 2019

Continuing Education

▸ This course provides education credits for the following certifications:
  ◦ Continuing Certification for PMPs & PMI-ACPs: 14 PDUs Category B: Continuing Education
  ◦ PMI-ACP Application: 14 Agile Education Contact Hours
  ◦ Scrum Alliance SEUs for CSP Application and Maintenance: 14 SEUS Category C: Outside Events
  ◦ Certified Business Analysis Professional (CBAP): 14 Hours of Professional Development

7

CAPE PROJECT MANAGEMENT, INC.

Product Owner Course Objectives

▸ Provide a review of the Scrum Framework
▸ Review in-depth the role of the Product Owner
▸ Gain a thorough understanding of the use of User Stories
▸ Prepare for the PSPO 1 Exam from Scrum.org
▸ Have fun!

8

CAPE PROJECT MANAGEMENT, INC.

Agenda

Day 1 – Modules	Day 2 – Modules
1. Introduction to Agile	6. The Agile Product Lifecycle
2. Scrum Framework	7. Agile Requirements
3. Scrum Roles	8. Agile Prioritizing
4. Scrum Events	9. Agile Sizing and Estimating
5. Scrum Artifacts	10. Agile Controls
The Sprint Game	11. Implementing Agile

9   Copyrighted material. 2019

Announcements

▶ Materials
- Slides
- Exercises
- List of Actual User Stories
- Glossary
- Group Activities
- Games

▶ Breaks

10   Copyrighted material. 2019

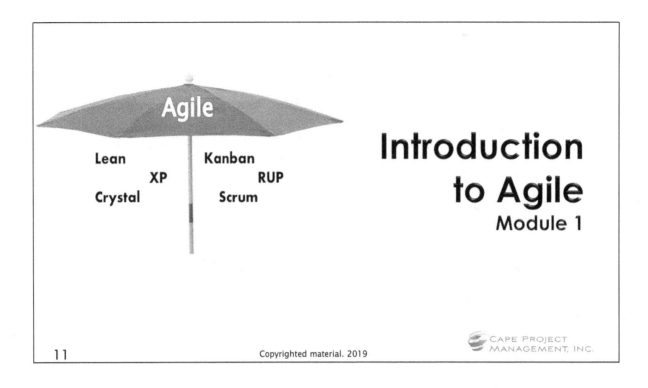

Introduction to Agile
Module 1

11

DISCUSSION

Why do projects fail?

12

Typical Project Risks

- Misunderstanding of the requirements
- Lack of management commitment and support
- Lack of adequate user involvement
- Failure to gain user commitment
- Failure to manage end user expectation
- Changes to requirements
- Lack of an effective project management methodology

http://mooc.ee/MTAT.03.243/2015_spring/uploads/Main/top-10.pdf

13

CAPE PROJECT
MANAGEMENT, INC.

Agile Project Management

- Agile is an umbrella term that encompasses many processes or methodologies.
- Common practices include Scrum, Extreme Programming, Adaptive System Development, DSDM, Feature Driven Development, Kanban, Crystal and more...

14

CAPE PROJECT
MANAGEMENT, INC.

Project Success Rates

	Successful	Challenged	Failed
Waterfall	11%	60%	29%
Agile	39%	52%	9%

■ Successful Challenged ■ Failed

Success = On-time, On-budget with a satisfactory result
(% of requirements met strategic goal)

https://www.infoq.com/articles/standish-chaos-2015

15

CAPE PROJECT
MANAGEMENT, INC.

Why is Agile more Successful?

16

CAPE PROJECT
MANAGEMENT, INC.

Requirements Stability vs. Development Approach

- Selecting a PMLC depends upon the stability of the requirements:
  - A predictive team can report exactly what features and tasks are planned for the entire length of the development process.
  - Adaptive methods focus on adapting quickly to changing realities. When the needs of a project change, an adaptive team changes as well.

Predictive   **Adaptive**

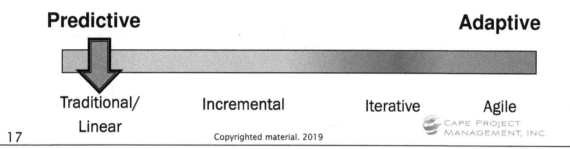

Traditional/ Linear   Incremental   Iterative   Agile

17

CAPE PROJECT MANAGEMENT, INC.

DISCUSSION

Why be more Agile or Adaptive in your organization?

What types of requirement changes do you experience?

18

CAPE PROJECT MANAGEMENT, INC.

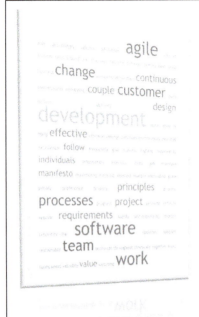

The
Agile Manifesto

19

20

The Agile Manifesto: A statement of values

We are uncovering better ways of developing software by doing it and helping others do it.

Through this work we have come to value:

Individuals and interactions	over	Process and tools
Working software	over	Comprehensive documentation
Customer collaboration	over	Contract negotiation
Responding to change	over	Following a plan

That is, while there is value in the items on the right, we value the items on the left more.

Source: www.agilemanifesto.org

CAPE PROJECT
MANAGEMENT, INC.

21

We value:

"Individuals and Interactions over processes and tools"

‣ The right people are more valuable than tools or methods

‣ New solutions and resolutions to problems are found through interactions and discussions

CAPE PROJECT
MANAGEMENT, INC.

22

We value:

"Working software over comprehensive documentation"

▸ The primary focus for software development teams must be on delivering something that works for the customer

▸ Documentation, though often necessary, needs to be prioritized, to those artifacts that provide value to the customer

CAPE PROJECT MANAGEMENT, INC.

We value:

"Customer Collaboration over contract negotiations"

▸ Listening to what the customer wants is more critical than meeting the language of a contract.

▸ Software development needs to be a collaboration between the user and the developer.

CAPE PROJECT MANAGEMENT, INC.

We value:

"Responding to change over following a plan"

▸ Plans are notoriously out of date as soon as they are written.

▸ By embracing change as opposed to trying to prevent it will deliver products that the customer is actually wanting.

25   Copyrighted material. 2019

---

12 Principles of the Agile Manifesto

1. Our highest priority is to satisfy the customer through early and continuous delivery of valuable software.

2. Welcome changing requirements, even late in development. Agile processes harness change for the customer's competitive advantage.

3. Deliver working software frequently, from a couple of weeks to a couple of months, with a preference to the shorter timescale.

4. Business people and developers must work together daily throughout the project.

5. Build projects around motivated individuals. Give them the environment and support they need, and trust them to get the job done.

6. The most efficient and effective method of conveying information to and within a development team is face-to-face conversation.

7. Working software is the primary measure of progress.

8. Agile processes promote sustainable development. The sponsors, developers, and users should be able to maintain a constant pace indefinitely.

9. Continuous attention to technical excellence and good design enhances agility.

10. Simplicity—the art of maximizing the amount of work not done—is essential.

11. The best architectures, requirements, and designs emerge from self-organizing teams.

12. At regular intervals, the team reflects on how to become more effective, then tunes and adjusts its behavior accordingly.

26   Copyrighted material. 2019

Activity: Agile Manifesto Principles

Directions:

1. Pair-up with another person at your table and review the Agile Manifesto Principles.
2. Pick three principles that you think are critical to the success of your Agile Implementation or are the most challenging.
3. Be prepared to share your answer with the class.

Principle	Choose 3
1. Our highest priority is to satisfy the customer through early and continuous delivery of valuable software.	
2. Welcome changing requirements, even late in development. Agile processes harness change for the customer's competitive advantage.	
3. Deliver working software frequently, from a couple of weeks to a couple of months, with a preference to the shorter timescale.	
4. Business people and developers must work together daily throughout the project.	
5. Build projects around motivated individuals. Give them the environment and support they need, and trust them to get the job done.	
6. The most efficient and effective method of conveying information to and within a development team is face-to-face conversation.	
7. Working software is the primary measure of progress.	

8. Agile processes promote sustainable development. The sponsors, developers, and users should be able to maintain a constant pace indefinitely.	
9. Continuous attention to technical excellence and good design enhances agility.	
10. Simplicity--the art of maximizing the amount of work not done--is essential.	
11. The best architectures, requirements, and designs emerge from self-organizing teams.	
12. At regular intervals, the team reflects on how to become more effective, then tunes and adjusts its behavior accordingly.	

Notes:

_____

_____

_____

_____

_____

_____

_____

Activity

Exercise 1:
Your 3 Principles

27   Copyrighted material. 2019   CAPE PROJECT MANAGEMENT, INC.

The Scrum Framework
Module 2

28   Copyrighted material. 2019   CAPE PROJECT MANAGEMENT, INC.

Scrum

▸ Scrum (n): A framework within which people can address complex adaptive problems, while productively and creatively delivering products of the highest possible value.

Source: Schwaber, Sutherland: *A Scrum Guide*

29   Copyrighted material. 2019

Origins of the idea

"The… 'relay race' approach to product development…may conflict with the goals of maximum speed and flexibility. Instead a holistic or 'rugby' approach—where a team tries to go the distance as a unit, passing the ball back and forth—may better serve today's competitive requirements."

Source: Hirotaka Takeuchi and Ikujiro Nonaka, "The New New Product Development Game", *Harvard Business Review*, January 1986.

30   Copyrighted material. 2019

Sequential vs. overlapping development

| Requirements | Design | Code | Test |

Rather than doing all of one thing at a time...

...Scrum teams do a little of everything all the time

Source: "The New New Product Development Game" by Takeuchi and Nonaka. *Harvard Business Review,* January 1986.

31

Copyrighted material. 2019

CAPE PROJECT
MANAGEMENT, INC.

History of Scrum

- Ken Schwaber and Jeff Sutherland developed the Scrum method and presented at a conference in 1996
- In 2002 "Agile Software Development with Scrum" was written by Ken Schwaber & Mike Beedle
- The Scrum method has evolved somewhat over the years.
- 2002 – Present, organic growth due to its anecdotal successes, grass roots adoption and an aggressive training approach have made it the most common Agile methodology
- The definitive guide to the rules of Scrum, *The Scrum Guide*, is maintained by Ken Schwaber and Jeff Sutherland. http://www.Scrumguides.org

32

Copyrighted material. 2019

CAPE PROJECT
MANAGEMENT, INC.

Scrum is:

- Scrum is a lightweight, simple to understand (but difficult to master) agile process framework.
- Scrum and Extreme Programming (XP) are two of the best-known Agile methods. XP emphasizes technical practices such as pair programming and continuous integration. Scrum emphasizes management practices such as the role of Scrum Master.
- Many companies use the management practices of Scrum with the technical practices of XP.
- Scrum is one of many different agile software development methods.

33   Copyrighted material. 2019   CAPE PROJECT MANAGEMENT, INC.

Scrum is Agile

Agile Frameworks
- XP
- Lean
- DSDM
- FDD
- Crystal Clear
- SaFE
- RUP

Scrum

34   Copyrighted material. 2019   CAPE PROJECT MANAGEMENT, INC.

3 Pillars of Scrum

Transparency
- ALL relative aspects of the process must be visible to those responsible for the outcome.

Inspection
- There is frequent inspection of the artifacts and progress to identify and correct undesirable variances. Inspection occurs during the Sprint Planning Meeting, Daily Scrum, Sprint Review and Sprint Retrospective.

Adaptation
- After inspection, adjustments should be made to the processes and artifacts to minimize further deviation.

5 Core Values of Scrum

1. **Commitment** – When we, as a team, value the **Commitment** we make to ourselves and our teammates, we are much more likely to give our all to meet our goals.

2. **Focus** – When we value **Focus**, and devote the whole of our attention to only a few things at once, we deliver a better quality product, faster.

3. **Openness** – When we value being **Open** with ourselves and our teammates, we feel comfortable inspecting our behavior and practices, we can adapt them accordingly.

4. **Respect** – When we value **Respect**, people feel safe to voice concerns and discuss issues, knowing that their voices are heard and valued.

5. **Courage** – When we value **Courage**, people are encouraged to step outside of their comfort zones and take on greater challenges, knowing they will not be punished if they fail.

41

42

Scrum Master Responsibilities

Ensures Backlog refinement occurs

Facilitates and ensures time-box

Expedites Issues and Facilitates Resolution

Scrum

Product Backlog

Sprint Backlog

Sprint

Working Software

Schedules meetings, manages time-box, supports estimation and prioritization.

43

CAPE PROJECT MANAGEMENT, INC.

The Scrum Master Dos

- Represents management to the project
- Responsible for enacting Scrum values and practices
- Removes impediments
- Ensure that the team is fully functional and productive
- Enable close cooperation across all roles and functions
- Shield the team from external interferences
- Is a Servant Leader

44

CAPE PROJECT MANAGEMENT, INC.

Servant Leadership

▸ Critical to building self-organizing teams
▸ More difficult, but more rewarding
▸ Facilitates the team to address the tasks
▸ Fosters an environment that is trusting and respectful; supports collaboration

CAPE PROJECT
MANAGEMENT, INC.

Servant Leadership

▸ Traditional leadership is "command-and-control"
  ◦ "Workers need to be monitored closely"
▸ Servant leadership is based upon trust
  ◦ "Team members are self-motivated"
▸ An agile servant leader needs to:
  ◦ Protect the team from outside distractions
  ◦ Remove impediments to the team's performance
  ◦ Communicate and re-communicate project vision
  ◦ "Move boulders and carry water"—in other words, remove obstacles that prevent the team from providing business value

CAPE PROJECT
MANAGEMENT, INC.

Scrum Master Don'ts

- Own the product decisions on Product Owner's behalf
- Estimate on team's behalf
- Make the technology decisions on team's behalf
- Assign the tasks to the team members
- Try to manage the team

Copyrighted material. 2019

CAPE PROJECT MANAGEMENT, INC.

Scrum Master – Top 5

1. Coach team members
2. Manage conflict
3. Facilitate decision making
4. Remove team impediments
5. Increase organizational awareness of Scrum

Copyrighted material. 2019

CAPE PROJECT MANAGEMENT, INC.

Product Owner Responsibilities

Listen and Answer Questions

Be available to answer questions and clarify details on...

Create and maintain the product backlog

Evaluate product at end of Sprint and add or remove stories from backlog as necessary

Product Backlog

Sprint Backlog

Scrum

Sprint

Working Software

Organize the backlog into incremental releases

Specify acceptance criteria for stories

Verify stories are done based on acceptance criteria

49

Copyrighted material. 2019

CAPE PROJECT MANAGEMENT, INC.

Product Owner Dos

- Define the features of the product
- Decide on release dates and content
- Be responsible the total cost of ownership (TCO) and the profitability of the product (ROI)
- Orders features according to market value
- Adjust features and priority every Sprint, as needed
- Available daily* to answer questions for the Development Team

*not necessarily full-time, but as needed

50

Copyrighted material. 2019

CAPE PROJECT MANAGEMENT, INC.

The Product Owner Is a:

- Subject Matter Expert
  - Understand the domain well enough to envision a product
  - Answer questions on the domain for those creating the product
- End User and Customer Advocate
  - Describe the product with understanding of users and its use.
  - Understand the needs of the business and select a mix of features valuable to the customer
- Business Advocate
  - Understand the needs of the organization paying for the software's construction and select a mix of features that serve their goals
- Communicator
  - Capable of communicating vision and intent – deferring detailed feature and design decisions to be made just in time
- Decision Maker
  - Given a variety of conflicting goals and opinions, be the final decision maker for hard product decisions

The Product Owner role is generally filled by a single person supported by a collaborative team

CAPE PROJECT
MANAGEMENT, INC.

51

Product Owner Interactions

CAPE PROJECT
MANAGEMENT, INC.

52

Product Owner Don'ts

- Choose how much work will be accomplished in the Sprint - the team will do this, based on the priorities
- Change anything within the Sprint once it has started and don't add items unless the Sprint will end early
- Answer the three questions at the Daily Scrum Meetings (unless they have a task on a User Story)

53 Copyrighted material. 2019

Product Owner – Top 5

1. Maximizes the value of the product backlog
2. Represent the customer in Scrum events
3. Ensure the team is adapting to change
4. Inspect product progress
5. Accept or reject work results

54 Copyrighted material. 2019

Product Owner vs Scrum Master

Two different roles that complement each other. If one is not played properly, the other suffers.

▸ The Product Owner is responsible for the **product success** (value)

▸ The Scrum Master is responsible for **project success** (team performance)

Copyrighted material. 2019

© Scott Adams, Inc./Dist. by UFS, Inc.

Copyrighted material. 2019

Team Responsibilities

Answers the 3 questions

Performs all activities needed to meet the POs requirements

Review the product backlog in advance of planning.

Delivers a finished product

Product Backlog

Sprint Backlog

Scrum

Sprint

Working Software

Decides what work they can complete in the Sprint

57

CAPE PROJECT MANAGEMENT, INC.

The Team Dos

▸ Typically 6 ± 3 people
▸ Teams are self-organizing
▸ Cross-functional:
  ◦ Programmers, testers, user experience designers, etc.
▸ Members should be full-time
  · May be exceptions (e.g., database administrator)
▸ Membership should change only between Sprints

58

 CAPE PROJECT MANAGEMENT, INC.

The Team Don'ts

‣ Skip Scrum Meetings

‣ Stop working when there is a roadblock or not enough information

‣ Increase technical debt in order to meet the velocity

‣ Individuals on a Scrum team should not do excessive individual overtime, or in any other way try to be the "hero" of the team.

   ◦ Scrum helps us build *great teams of people, not teams of great people*
   ~ Barry Turner

59

CAPE PROJECT
MANAGEMENT, INC.

What is a self-organizing team?

‣ Team members are self-empowered (they know what needs to be done and have the means to do it)

‣ They are willing to take on the responsibility of self-organizing and self-examining

‣ They are ready to let go of their individual egos and differences so that the team can function together

‣ Scrum's success is dependent on the team's ability to self-examine itself and to continually seek improvement

http://blog.openviewpartners.com/scrum-challenge-self-organizing-teams/

60

CAPE PROJECT
MANAGEMENT, INC.

61

The Team Top 5

1. Self-organizing team members have to be more creative
2. Have to have a strong discipline and work ethic
3. Must be committed to the project's goals
4. Respect each other
5. Share a genuine conviction that the "we"—the potent concept behind every team—will succeed or fail together

62

How Teams Develop

Forming

Storming

Norming

Performing

Source: Bruce Tuckman: "Developmental sequence in small groups"

CAPE PROJECT
MANAGEMENT, INC.

63 Copyrighted material. 2019

Forming

▸ In this stage, most team members are positive and polite. Some are anxious, as they haven't fully understood what work the team will do. Others are simply excited about the task ahead.

▸ The leader will play a dominant role at this stage, because team members' roles and responsibilities aren't clear.

▸ This stage can last for some time, as people start to work together, and as they make an effort to get to know their new colleagues.

CAPE PROJECT
MANAGEMENT, INC.

64 Copyrighted material. 2019

Storming

- This is the stage where many teams fail.
- Storming often starts where there is a conflict between team members' natural working styles.
- If it has not been clearly defined how the team will work, people may feel overwhelmed by their workload.
- Some people may question the worth of the team's goal, and they may resist taking on tasks.
- Team members who stick with the task at hand may experience stress, particularly as they don't have the support of established processes, or strong relationships with their colleagues.

65 Copyrighted material. 2019   CAPE PROJECT MANAGEMENT, INC.

Norming

- This is when people start to resolve their differences, appreciate colleagues' strengths, and respect the leader.
- Now that the team members know one another better, they may socialize together, and they are able to ask each other for help and provide constructive feedback.
- People develop a stronger commitment to the team goal, and start to see good progress towards it.
- There is often a prolonged overlap between storming and norming, because, as new tasks come up, the team may lapse back into behavior from the storming stage.

66 Copyrighted material. 2019   CAPE PROJECT MANAGEMENT, INC.

Performing

- ▸ The team reaches the performing stage when hard work and minimal friction leads to the achievement of the team's goal.
- ▸ The structures and processes set up support this well.
- ▸ The leader can concentrate on developing individual team members.
- ▸ It feels easy to be part of the team at this stage, and people who join or leave won't disrupt performance.

 CAPE PROJECT MANAGEMENT, INC.

DISCUSSION

Have you ever been on a high-performing team? What were some of the attributes?

  CAPE PROJECT MANAGEMENT, INC.

Attributes of a High-performing Team

Excerpted from The Collaboration Imperative by Ron Ricci and Carl Wiese.

69

Team Communication in Agile

▸ Face-to-face
▸ Osmotic communication
▸ Open Spaces
▸ Distributed teams

70

Face-to-Face Communication

"The most efficient and effective method of conveying information to and within a development team is face-to-face conversation."
– the Agile Manifesto

▸ Co-located teams benefits from this type of communication
▸ User story creation with team members present is highly desirable
▸ Providing feedback during the Sprint would be desirable face-to face

71

CAPE PROJECT
MANAGEMENT, INC.

Face-To-Face Communication

72

CAPE PROJECT
MANAGEMENT, INC.

Osmotic Communication

- The basis of the open workspace model
- Information flows into the background hearing of team members
- Pick up relevant information as though by osmosis
- Supports fewer meetings
- Studies show double the productivity and decreased time to market

73

CAPE PROJECT
MANAGEMENT, INC.

Open Space Design

http://jamesshore.com/Agile-Book/sit_together.html

74

CAPE PROJECT
MANAGEMENT, INC.

Exercise: Scrum Ownership

	Team	Product Owner	Scrum Master
Provides Estimates			
Prioritizes Backlog			
Creates Requirements			
Commits To The Sprint			
Performs User Acceptance			
Facilitates Meetings			
Champion Of Scrum			
Volunteers For Tasks			
Makes Technical Decisions			
Designs Software			
Removes Impediments			
Defines Done			
Assign Tasks			

Activity

Exercise 2:
Scrum Ownership

75

CAPE PROJECT
MANAGEMENT, INC.

Fist of Five
Scrum Roles versus Scrum-Buts

76

CAPE PROJECT
MANAGEMENT, INC.

77

78

Scrum Events

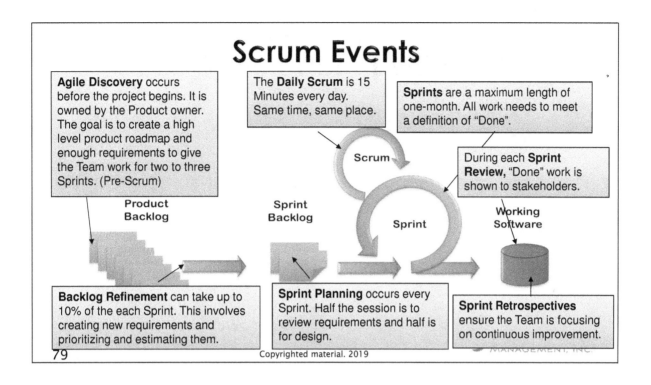

Agile Discovery occurs before the project begins. It is owned by the Product owner. The goal is to create a high level product roadmap and enough requirements to give the Team work for two to three Sprints. (Pre-Scrum)

The **Daily Scrum** is 15 Minutes every day. Same time, same place.

Sprints are a maximum length of one-month. All work needs to meet a definition of "Done".

During each **Sprint Review,** "Done" work is shown to stakeholders.

Backlog Refinement can take up to 10% of the each Sprint. This involves creating new requirements and prioritizing and estimating them.

Sprint Planning occurs every Sprint. Half the session is to review requirements and half is for design.

Sprint Retrospectives ensure the Team is focusing on continuous improvement.

79

The Scrum Events

Events	Timebox
Sprint Planning	8 hours for a one-month sprint • 1 hour/week of Sprint on requirements • 1 hour/week of Sprint on design
Sprints	One-month maximum
Daily Scrum	15 minutes daily
Backlog Refinement	2 hours per week (recommendation)
Sprint Review	4 hours for a one-month sprint • 1 hour/week of Sprint • 1 hour prep
Sprint Retrospectives	3 hours for a one-month sprint

CAPE PROJECT
MANAGEMENT, INC.

80

Why Timeboxing?

Sprint Planning

Part 1: Requirements Workshop	Part 2: Design Session
▸ 4 hours*	▸ 4 hours*
▸ Scrum Team	▸ Product Owner is optional but available
▸ Sprint Backlog prioritization	▸ Design/Task Definition
▸ Define "Done" (first Sprint)	▸ Re-estimate?
▸ Estimate User Stories	▸ Re-prioritize?

First day of the Sprint
*1 hour per week of Sprint

* For a one-month Sprint

83　Copyrighted material. 2019

The Sprint Goal

▸ A sprint goal is a short, one- or two-sentence, description of what the team plans to achieve during the sprint. It is written collaboratively by the team and the product owner.

▸ The following are example sprint goals on an eCommerce application:
  ◦ Implement basic shopping cart functionality including add, remove, and update quantities.
  ◦ Develop the checkout process: pay for an order, pick shipping, order gift wrapping, etc.

▸ The success of the sprint will later be assessed during the sprint review meeting against the sprint goal, rather than against each specific item selected from the product backlog.

84　Copyrighted material. 2019

Effective Sprint Planning Meetings

- Start the meeting with a roadmap review
- The Product Owner needs to be able to articulate a Sprint objective
- The team decides when the User Stories (requirements) are "good enough" e.g. Definition of Ready
- Backlog refinement is performed in advance of at least two Sprints

CAPE PROJECT
MANAGEMENT, INC.

Backlog Refinement

- Each Sprint, the team and Product Owner collaborate to add detail, estimates, and order to items in the Product Backlog.
- Refinement usually consumes no more than 10% of the capacity of the Development Team. Unique to Agile
- Product Owner, Scrum Master, and Dev Team decides how and when refinement is done.
- The Product Backlog items can be updated at any time by the Product Owner

CAPE PROJECT
MANAGEMENT, INC.

Backlog Refinement Tips

- Try to never schedule backlog refinement during the first or last 20% of the Sprint.
- Treat the backlog refinement meeting just like the first part of the Sprint Planning Meeting
- The Product Owner should present enough work to plan 2 Sprints beyond the current Sprint.
- Allow Story Splitting and Sizing to occur
- Make sure everyone understands that estimates are not final until Sprint Planning is performed

87   Copyrighted material. 2019

The Sprint

- Scrum projects progress via a series of Sprints.
- Each Sprint should produce "potentially releasable" functionality
- During a Sprint, the Scrum team takes a small set of features (an increment of work) from idea to coded and tested functionality.
- At the end of the Sprint, these features meet an agreed upon definition of "Done"
- Each Sprint immediately follows the previous one
- Sprint lengths are determined by the following criteria:
  ○ No more than one calendar month
  ○ Not so long that the risk is unacceptable to the Product Owner.
  ○ Not so short that other business events can't be readily synchronized with the development work.

88   Copyrighted material. 2019

What is the Definition of Done?

▸ Defined collaboratively by Product Owner and Development Team
▸ Ensures product is ready for release whether internally to another department or externally
▸ Considerations
  ◦ Functionality, Quality, Coding standards, Test coverage, Integration testing, Documented
▸ Risks of unclear definition of done
  ◦ Inaccurate Velocity
  ◦ Technical debt
▸ 0/100% Rule (if it is not done, it doesn't count)

89

No changes during a Sprint

Plan Sprint durations around how long the Product Owner can commit to keeping change out of the Sprint

90

Four-week Sprint

Pros:

▸ **Very easy to roadmap.** Long-term, one-year roadmaps are much easier when you only have to plan 12 iterations.

▸ **Low process load.** The key Scrum meetings only once per month, your team is spending less time in meetings and more time building.

Cons:

▸ **Long turnaround time.** A new idea that comes in the day after a Sprint kickoff can't be started for a month and wouldn't be demoed until a month after that. Two months turnaround time from request to demo can feel interminable.

▸ **Mini-waterfall.** There is a risk on a four-week Sprint to break up the weeks into design, develop, test, integrate.

One-week Sprint

Pros:

▸ **Fast turnaround time.** At most, a new idea has to wait just a week to start development and a week after that for the first product output.

▸ **High energy.** One-week Sprints are fun. The energy is high because the deadline is always this Friday. Every week is an end-of-Sprint rush to the finish line.

Cons:

▸ **Minimal feedback.** There isn't time for a lot of customer feedback before delivering code.

▸ **Lack of a roadmap.** When your horizon is a week it is difficult planning out a year.

▸ **Story sizing.** It can be difficult to size all Stories to fit into a week.

▸ **Relatively heavy...or no process.** A one-week Sprint still needs estimation, tasking, demo, refinement, etc. Relative to the size of the Sprint those fixed time costs will now be high. In practice, the Sprint processes get rushed or omitted.

DISCUSSION

What is the right Sprint length for you organization?

Copyrighted material. 2019

The Daily Scrum

▸ Parameters
  ◦ Daily
  ◦ Same time
  ◦ 15-minutes
  ◦ Stand-up (optional)
▸ Not for problem solving
  ◦ Whole world is invited
  ◦ Only team members and Scrum Master can talk
▸ Helps avoid other unnecessary meetings

94 Copyrighted material. 2019

Purpose of the Daily Scrum

- To help start the day well
- To support improvement
- To reinforce focus on the right things
- To reinforce the sense of team
- To communicate what is going on

CAPE PROJECT MANAGEMENT, INC.

Everyone answers 3 questions

1 What did you do yesterday?

2 What will you do today?

3 Is anything in your way?

- These are *not* a status for the Scrum Master
  - They are commitments in front of peers

CAPE PROJECT MANAGEMENT, INC.

Sprint Review Meeting

- Time-boxed—one hour per each week of Sprint
- One-hour prep
- Only "done" items are demonstrated
  ◦ Done versus done-done
- Opportunity for "inspect and adapt"
- Primary audience are stakeholders
- Feedback is encouraged

CAPE PROJECT MANAGEMENT, INC.

Sprint Review Do's and Don'ts

Do's
- Ensure it is the Product Owner's meeting
- Show the progress against the Product Backlog & Roadmap
- Make certain stakeholders are present
- Prepare in advance
- Team members present the content

Don'ts
- The Product Owner acts as customer (they should not be seeing anything for the first time)
- Allow Sprint Reviews to become boring meetings
- Not showing working and tested software

CAPE PROJECT MANAGEMENT, INC.

Sprint Retrospective Meeting

- ▸ Periodically take a look at what is and is not working
- ▸ Only attended by the Scrum Team (no stakeholders)
- ▸ Done after every Sprint
- ▸ Time-boxed: 3 hours for a one month Sprint
- ▸ Use a neutral facilitator
- ▸ Important to have open feedback
- ▸ Incorporate feedback into next Sprint

99

Copyrighted material. 2019

 CAPE PROJECT
MANAGEMENT, INC.

Sprint Retrospectives

- ▸ Examines the way work was performed
- ▸ Inspects how the last Sprint went in terms of people, relationships, process, and tools
- ▸ Identifies and prioritizes the major items that went well as well as potential improvements
- ▸ Creates a plan for implementing improvements to the way the Team does its work

100

Copyrighted material. 2019

CAPE PROJECT
MANAGEMENT, INC.

Start / Stop / Continue

▸ Whole team gathers and discusses what they'd like to:

Start doing

Stop doing

Continue doing

This is just one of many ways to do a Sprint Retrospective.

101   Copyrighted material. 2019

DISCUSSION

Which ritual is easiest?
Which is hardest?

102   Copyrighted material. 2019

Sample end of Sprint agenda – The "Planning Day"

Time	Item (two week Sprint)
9:00–9:15	Daily Scrum • Last Scrum of prior Sprint-discuss status of any incomplete stories
9:15–10:30	Sprint Review: • Demo of stories delivered over the course of last Sprint
10:30–11:30	Sprint Retrospective • Focus both on product and process opportunities
11:30–12:30	Lunch
12:30 – 2:30	Sprint Planning Requirements Session: • Review roadmap, discuss sprint goal, review each story in priority order and estimate until velocity is met
2:30–4:30	Sprint Planning Design Session: • Team reviews stories, creates tasks for each
4:30–4:45	Team commits to the Sprint Backlog • Ready to start with a daily Scrum the next day

103 CAPE PROJECT MANAGEMENT, INC.

Summary: PO Role by Event

Events	Responsibility
Sprint Planning	Be prepared with a Sprint Objective and proposed Sprint Backlog
Sprints	Be available daily to answer questions, elaborate on requirements and accept or reject stories.
Daily Scrum	Listen and answer questions.
Backlog Refinement	Review backlog with team up to 2 Sprints ahead for estimation and prioritization.
Sprint Review	Ensure stakeholders attend. Present progress against roadmap, and provide forum for inspect and adapt.
Sprint Retrospectives	Attend as a team member.

104 CAPE PROJECT MANAGEMENT, INC.

Scaling Scrum

- Productivity comes from small teams
- Factors in scaling
  - ◦ Team size
  - ◦ Type of application
  - ◦ Team dispersion
  - ◦ Features
- Scrum has been used on multiple 500+ person projects
- Management may require a Scrum of Scrums
- Risk: healthcare.gov

105   Copyrighted material. 2019

CAPE PROJECT
MANAGEMENT, INC.

Productivity vs. Team Size

Number of People	Time (in months)
1.5–3	13.6

Source: http://www.qsm.com/process_improvement_01.html

106   Copyrighted material. 2019

CAPE PROJECT
MANAGEMENT, INC.

Program Management via Scrum of Scrums

Chief Scrum Master: Release
Training Engineer (RTE)

Copyrighted material. 2019

CAPE PROJECT
MANAGEMENT, INC.

Scrum of Scrums

- Supports multiple teams working on the same product with the intent to address dependent issues
- Each team identifies one person who attends the Scrum of Scrums, usually the Scrum Master.
- The RTE maintains a backlog of issues and problems to address
- A Scrum of Scrums meets two or three times a week
- Scrum of Scrums Questions:
  - What has your team done since we last met?
  - What will your team do before we meet again?
  - Is anything slowing your team down or getting in their way?
  - Are you about to put something in another team's way?

Copyrighted material. 2019

CAPE PROJECT
MANAGEMENT, INC.

Scaling and the Product Owner Role

- Typically, a product owner cannot look after more than two - three teams.
- The solution is to introduce a Chief Product Owner Product Manager who is responsible for the overall product.
- The Chief Product Owner has content authority for the Program Backlog. They are responsible for identifying customer needs, prioritizing features, guiding the work and developing the program vision and roadmap.
- In order to manage the product, we can divide the product by features, sub products, lines of business.

 CAPE PROJECT MANAGEMENT, INC.

Scaling the Product Owner Role

 CAPE PROJECT MANAGEMENT, INC.

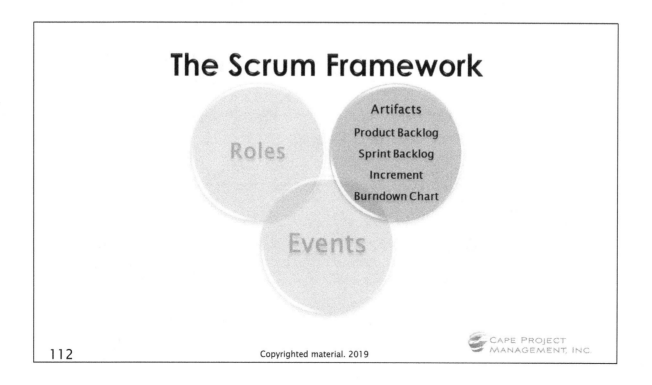

Information Radiators

- Publically posted information
- Easy to read
- Can be understood at a glance
- Can change frequently
- Easy to manage
- Examples:
  - War Rooms
  - Backlogs
  - Burndown Charts

 CAPE PROJECT MANAGEMENT, INC.

Artifact 1: Product Backlog

- The requirements
- A list of all desired work on the project
- Product Backlog items have the attributes of a description, order, estimate and value.
- Prioritized by the product owner
- Reprioritized at the start of each Sprint

 CAPE PROJECT MANAGEMENT, INC.

Copyrighted material. 2019

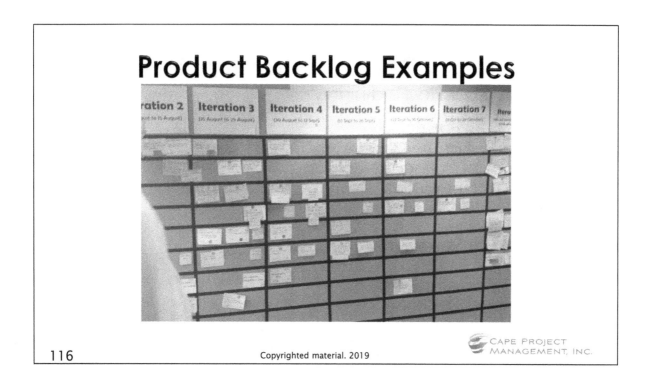

Copyrighted material. 2019

Product Backlog Examples

CAPE PROJECT
MANAGEMENT, INC.

Artifact 2: The Sprint Backlog

▸ The Sprint Backlog is a highly visible, real-time picture of the work that the Development Team plans to accomplish during the Sprint, and it belongs solely to the Development Team.
    ~ Scrum Guide

▸ Created at Sprint Planning Meeting
▸ Based upon story size, priority and velocity

CAPE PROJECT
MANAGEMENT, INC.

The Sprint Backlog is Emergent

- ▸ Work is added as needed to meet the Sprint Goal
- ▸ Can be additional backlog items or tasks
- ▸ Belongs solely to the Development Team.

Sprint Backlog

Sprint Backlog	In Progress	Completed (Done)

Sprint Backlog

CAPE PROJECT MANAGEMENT, INC.

Artifact 3: The Increment

- The Increment is the sum of all the Product Backlog items completed during a Sprint and the value of the increments of all previous Sprints.
- At the end of a Sprint, the new Increment must be "Done," which means it must be in useable condition and meet the Scrum Team's definition of "Done."
- It must be in useable condition regardless of whether the Product Owner decides to actually release it.

CAPE PROJECT MANAGEMENT, INC.

Optional Artifact: The Burndown Chart

- Tracks work remaining over time
- At-a-glance information
  - Duration of Sprint
  - Target velocity
  - Performance against plan
    - Above the line– behind schedule
    - Below the line – ahead of schedule
- Sprint burndown
- Release burndown

Copyrighted material. 2019

CAPE PROJECT MANAGEMENT, INC.

Velocity

- Velocity = Rate of Progress
- Number of story points to be completed in Sprint
- First Sprint is a guess
- Estimate improves over time
- Account for work done and disruptions on the project
- Based upon team synergy

Copyrighted material. 2019

CAPE PROJECT MANAGEMENT, INC.

131

132

GROUP EXERCISE

The Sprint Game

133

The Goal

- Accomplish as many of the User Stories you have been given based upon a release plan of 3-5 iterations (Sprints)
- To accomplish this, you will:
  - Prioritize requirements (User Stories)
  - Estimate the size of the User Stories using Story Points
  - Create and execute the plan for the first Sprint
  - Retrospect and plan the next Sprint
  - Track your results and plan using velocity
  - Repeat
- Everyone has to commit!

134

Step 1: Backlog Refinement
20 Minutes

- The Product Owner provides User Story cards
- The Team estimates complexity of all of the User Stories using T-Shirt Sizes and writes the size on the User Story card.
- The Team orders the Product Backlog by relative priority from largest to smallest using this formula:

X-small	1 Story Point
Small	3 Story Points
Medium	5 Story Points
Large	8 Story Points
X-large	13 Story Points
XX-large	Impossible

$$\frac{Priority}{Size} = Relative\ Priority$$

135

CAPE PROJECT MANAGEMENT, INC.

Step 2: Create your Sprint Plan
5 Minutes

- Starting with the highest priority Stories on the Product Backlog and select which ones you can complete in a 3 minute Sprint (Sprint Backlog)
- Total the number of Story Points you expect to complete in the Sprint Backlog (Target Velocity)
- Document the Target Velocity on the Sprint Burnup
- Acquire all of the resources you need to execute your Sprint (cards, balloons, etc.)

136

CAPE PROJECT MANAGEMENT, INC.

Step 3: Sprint
3 Minutes

▸ Execute your User Stories

▸ Acceptance can occur during the Sprint

▸ If you finish early, the you can pick additional User Stories from the Product Backlog

▸ If a story goes badly, you may abandon it...
  ◦ ... if your Product Owner agrees

137

Step 4: Inspect and Adapt, Plan, Repeat
5 minutes

▸ Document Actual Velocity on Burnup chart and re-plan the next Sprint

▸ Review and validate estimates

▸ Determine new velocity – yesterday's weather

▸ Document Target and Actual Velocity on Sprint Burnup chart

138

Retrospective

▸ What did you learn?

▸ What would you do differently?

139
Copyrighted material. 2019

CAPE PROJECT
MANAGEMENT, INC.

BE AGILE®

Product Owner and User Story Training

Day 2

CAPE PROJECT
MANAGEMENT, INC.

GROUP EXERCISE

Scrum Review
Who wants to be an Agile Millionaire!

http://bit.ly/ScrumGames

(Agile Onion)

The Agile Product Lifecycle
Module 1

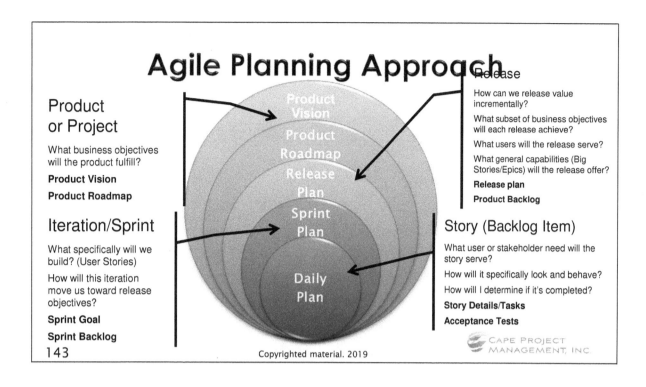

Agile Plans

▸ Typically are top-down
▸ Are easy to change
▸ Limit dependencies
▸ Follow a rolling-wave approach
  ◦ Rolling Wave Planning is a technique that enables you to plan for a project as it unfolds. This technique requires you to plan iteratively. You plan until you have more visibility and then re-plan.

145

CAPE PROJECT
MANAGEMENT, INC.

Creating a Product Vision

Product Vision

146

CAPE PROJECT
MANAGEMENT, INC.

Developing a Vision

▸ The product vision is key to the success of the project.

▸ The product vision should align with the company vision

▸ The vision should be revisited frequently

▸ All releases of the product should related back to the vision

CAPE PROJECT
MANAGEMENT, INC.

147

Effective Vision Statements

| Concise

| Clear

| Communicated

| Compelling

| Contagious

CAPE PROJECT
MANAGEMENT, INC.

148

Effective Vision Statements

▸ **Concise**: An effective vision statement must be short and simple so it can be understood and articulated by everyone in the organization.

▸ **Clear**: Lack of clarity may be the single greatest failure of a healthy vision.

▸ **Communicated**: A vision statement can be concise and clear, but unless it is communicated well, it has little power.

▸ **Compelling**: You should be able to see clearly in the vision statement something that will naturally move people toward greater commitment and decisive actions.

▸ **Contagious**: The vision statement should be something that makes the organization proud.

149   Copyrighted material. 2019   CAPE PROJECT MANAGEMENT, INC.

Effective Vision Statements

"Our vision is to be earth's most customer centric company; to build a place where people can come to find and discover anything they might want to buy online."

"Making the best possible ice cream, in the nicest possible way"

"Give customers the freshest, highest quality foods you can buy and provide them with friendly service in a sparkling clean environment."

150   Copyrighted material. 2019   CAPE PROJECT MANAGEMENT, INC.

Company Vision vs. Product Vision

Company Vision
- Our goal is to make learning more desirable, accessible, and meaningful for learners. By doing this, we have a shared sense of purpose with teachers, administrators, and leaders at all levels that are working to improve outcomes for learners.

Product Vision
- The Learning Management System (LMS) will enhance the educational experience by giving students and educators more ways to stay engaged online - both in and outside of the classroom. It will give students and faculty access to their courses, content, and grading and will allow them to participate in an online learning community on their desktop and variety of mobile devices.

151
Copyrighted material. 2019
CAPE PROJECT MANAGEMENT, INC.

Create a Vision Board

Vision: What is your overarching goal for creating the product?			
Product	Needs	Target Group	Value
What is the product? What makes it desirable? Is it feasible to develop?	What problem does the product solve? What benefit does it provide?	Who are the target users and customers?	How is the product going to benefit the company? What are the business goals?

Source: http://www.romanpichler.com/blog/the-product-vision-board/

152
Copyrighted material. 2019
CAPE PROJECT MANAGEMENT, INC.

Vision Board Example

Vision: The Learning Management System (LMS) will enhance the educational experience by giving students and educators more ways to stay engaged online - both in and outside of the classroom. It will give students and faculty access to their courses, content, and grading and will allow them to participate in an online learning community on their desktop and variety of mobile devices.

Product	Needs	Target Group	Value
Online access to courses, grading, and student profiles. Eliminates paper and provides platform for collaboration. Development team and expertise exists.	Eliminates the need for paper catalogs, add/drop forms and high involvement of faculty. Reduces overhead, 24/7 access and ability to change content.	Students Faculty Administrators Parents	Customer base is every university, school, and training organization in the world. Generate revenue with each release of functionality.

153

CAPE PROJECT MANAGEMENT, INC.

GROUP EXERCISE

Exercise 3:
Create a Product Vision Board

154

CAPE PROJECT MANAGEMENT, INC.

Group Exercise: Create a Vision Board

1. Select a Case Study

    a. Provide a site to store all cross departmental documents, maintain public personnel profiles, support internal blogs, and provided external and public viewing of program status and progress against departmental objectives.

    b. Create a social networking site that combines the concept of Meetups, dating, and event planning for those people interested in outdoor activities.

    c. Design and build new cafeteria for your building that that meets the needs of your organization and is also a profit center to draw external customers.

2. Create a Vision Board with your team
3. Be prepared to share with the class

Product Name:

Vision Statement:

Product	Needs	Target Group	Value

Vision: What is your overarching goal for creating the product?

Product	Needs	Target Group	Value
What is the product? What makes it desirable? Is it feasible to develop?	What problem does the product solve? What benefit does it provide?	Who are the target users and customers?	How is the product going to benefit the company? What are the business goals?

Vision: The Learning Management System (LMS) will enhance the educational experience by giving students and educators more ways to stay engaged online - both in and outside of the classroom. It will give students and faculty access to their courses, content, and grading and will allow them to participate in an online learning community on their desktop and variety of mobile devices.

Product	Needs	Target Group	Value
Online access to courses, grading, and student profiles. Eliminates paper and provides platform for collaboration. Development team and expertise exists.	Eliminates the need for paper catalogs, add/drop forms and high involvement of faculty. Reduces overhead, 24/7 access and ability to change content.	Students Faculty Administrators Parents	Customer base is every university, school, and training organization in the world. Generate revenue with each release of functionality.

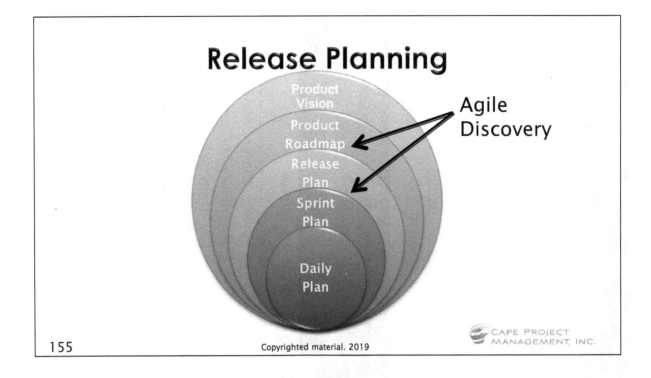

155

Agile Discovery

- **Desired Business Outcomes:** Document outcomes that are quantifiable and measurable.
- **High Level Architecture:** Outline a plan for the technical and business architecture/design of the solution.
- **High Level Delivery Plan:** Segment the solution into the smallest minimum viable products (MVPs) that realize the desired outcomes and sets out the order in which they are to be delivered.
- **Product Backlog:** Create an evolving prioritized list of all items of work which may be relevant to the solution.
- **Governance Approach:** Describe essential governance and organization aspects of the project and how the project will be managed.
- **High-Level Budget:** Create a project budget and release budget to support resource planning and scheduling.

156

Product Roadmap

- A roadmap is a planned future, laid out in broad strokes
  - Planned or proposed product releases, listing high level functionality or release themes, laid out in rough timeframes
  - For a period usually extending for 2 or 3 significant feature releases into the future
- Shows progress towards strategy
- Lots of "wiggle room"
- Example:
  - Implement course listing functionality
  - Implement grading functionality
  - Implement discussion groups
  - Implement student profiles

157   Copyrighted material. 2019

Release Options

- Organized around business value
- Internal release versus external release
- Daily builds and continuous integration versus planned release schedule

158   Copyrighted material. 2019

Minimum Viable Product (MVP)

▸ The product with the highest return on investment versus risk.

▸ Just those core features that allow the product to be deployed, and no more.

▸ It allows you to test an idea or hypothesis by exposing an early version of your product to the target users and customers, to collect the relevant data, and to learn from it.

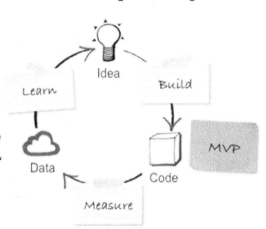

Source: http://www.romanpichler.com/blog/minimum-viable-product-and-minimal-marketable-product/

159   Copyrighted material. 2019   CAPE PROJECT MANAGEMENT, INC.

Types of Hypothesis

1. Problem hypothesis
   ○ We assume there a problem.

2. User hypothesis
   ○ We assume these people have this problem.

3. Solution hypothesis
   ○ We assume our solution will solve it.

4. Growth hypothesis
   ○ We assume there are enough users.

160   Copyrighted material. 2019   CAPE PROJECT MANAGEMENT, INC.

A Product Release Plan

▸ Goes into next level of detail
▸ Sets a common understanding
▸ A projection, not a commitment
▸ Example
  ◦ Release 1:
    • LMS Installed with pilot group logins validated
    • Pilot with 3 faculty and 60 students
    • Course listings available
  ◦ Release 2
    • Incorporate pilot feedback
    • Enable College of Engineering faculty and students
    • Implement course selection on-line
  ◦ Release 3
    • ...

161

CAPE PROJECT
MANAGEMENT, INC.

Product Roadmap & Release Plan

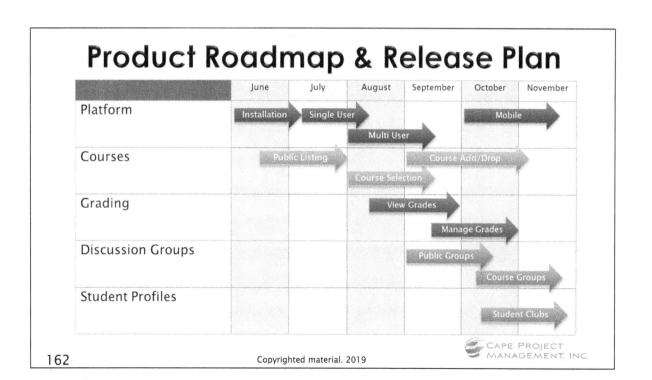

162

CAPE PROJECT
MANAGEMENT, INC.

CAPE PROJECT MANAGEMENT, INC.

Steps to User Story Mapping

1. Product Roadmap Definition
2. User Story Definition
3. User Story Decomposition
4. Release Planning

CAPE PROJECT MANAGEMENT, INC.

Step 1-Product Roadmap Definition

▸ Spatial arrangement:
- Lay out your product roadmap by major user stories, themes or epics
- Arrange them left to right in the order you want to make these stories available

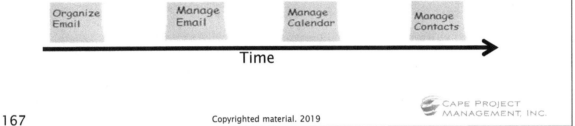

CAPE PROJECT MANAGEMENT, INC.

Step 2- User Story Definition

Create and arrange the user stories that will be performed within each epic or theme.

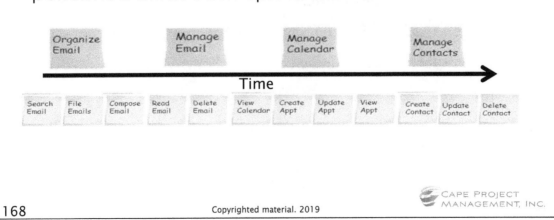

CAPE PROJECT MANAGEMENT, INC.

Step 3- User Story Decomposition

Identify additional user stories and tasks associated with each vertical slice of functionality

Below each activity, or large story are the child stories that make it up

169

CAPE PROJECT MANAGEMENT, INC.

Step 4 - Release Planning

- Prioritize user stories based on product roadmap and product goal
  - Product goals describe what outcome or benefit is received by the organization after the product is put into use
  - Use product goals to identify incremental releases, where each release delivers some benefit
- Create horizontal swim-lanes to group features into releases
- Arrange features vertically by priority from the user's perspective
- Split user stories into pieces that can be deferred until later releases

170

CAPE PROJECT MANAGEMENT, INC.

Step 4-Release Planning

Priority (vertical axis)

Organize Email					Manage Email		Manage Calendar			Manage Contacts		
Search Email	File Emails	Compose Email	Read Email	Delete Email	View Calendar	Create Appt	Update Appt	View Appt	Create Contact	Update Contact	Delete Contact

Release 1
- Search by Keyword (WIP)
- Move Emails
- Create and send basic email (Done)
- Open basic email (Done)
- Delete email
- View list of appts (Done)
- Create basic appt (Done)
- Update contents/location
- View Appt (Done)
- Create basic contact (Done)
- Update contact info (WIP)
- Create sub folders (Done)
- Send RTF e-mail
- Open RTF e-mail
- View Monthly formats (WIP)
- Create RTF appt
- Accept/Reject/Tentative

Release 2
- Limit Search to one field
- Send HTML e-mail
- Open HTML e-mail
- Empty Deleted Items
- View Daily Format
- Create HTML appt
- Propose new time
- Add address data
- Update Address Info
- Delete Contact
- Limit Search to 1+ fields
- Set email priority
- Open Attachments
- Mandatory/Optional

Release 3
- Search attachments
- Get address from contacts
- View Weekly Formats
- Get address from contacts
- View Attachments
- Import Contacts
- Search sub folders
- Send Attachments
- Search Calendar
- Add Attachments
- Export Contacts

Copyrighted material. 2019

CAPE PROJECT MANAGEMENT, INC.

GROUP EXERCISE

Exercise 4:
Roadmap & Release Plan
Define your MVP for 3-5 Releases

Copyrighted material. 2019

CAPE PROJECT MANAGEMENT, INC.

romanpichler

THE GO PRODUCT ROADMAP

	Date or timeframe	Date or timeframe	Date or timeframe	Date or timeframe
DATE The release date or timeframe				
NAME The name of the new release	Name/version	Name/version	Name/version	Name/version
GOAL The reason for creating the new release	Goal	Goal	Goal	Goal
FEATURES The high-level features necessary to meet the goal	Features	Features	Features	Features
METRICS The metrics to determine if the goal has been met	Metrics	Metrics	Metrics	Metrics

www.romanpichler.com
Template version 10/16

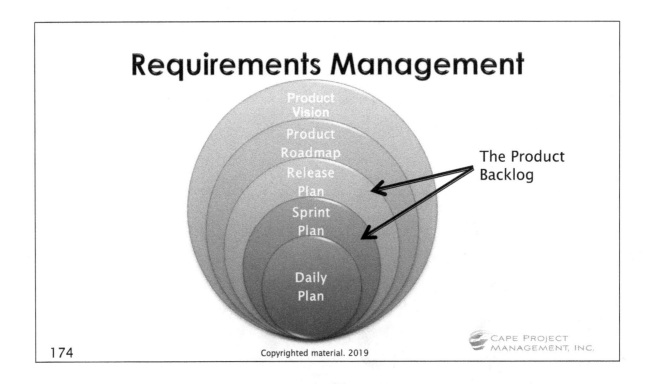

Product Owner's Role

- Single owner of the Product Backlog
- Maximizes the value (ROI) of the Product Backlog
- Determines how to order the Product Backlog but can delegate this function
- Ensures the Product Backlog is transparent to the entire organization
- Makes certain the backlog is "ready' for the Sprint Planning (otherwise Sprint is canceled)

175   Copyrighted material. 2019   CAPE PROJECT MANAGEMENT, INC.

Types of Backlogs

Type/View	Definition
Product	Set of prioritized requirements aligning with product vision
Release	The minimum requirements that would support a release. • Smallest possible release contains one Sprint • "Done-Done"
Sprint	A subset of requirements selected according to the velocity (capacity) of the team

176   Copyrighted material. 2019   CAPE PROJECT MANAGEMENT, INC.

Make the Product Backlog DEEP

▸ **Detailed Appropriately.** User stories on the product backlog that will be done soon need to be sufficiently well understood that they can be completed in the coming sprint. Stories to be developed later should be described with less detail.

▸ **Estimated.** The product backlog is more than a list of all work to be done; it is also a useful planning tool. Because items further down the backlog are not as well understood (yet), the estimates associated with them will be less precise than estimates given items at the top.

▸ **Emergent.** A product backlog is not static. It will change over time. As more is learned, user stories on the product backlog will be added, removed, or reprioritized.

▸ **Prioritized.** The product backlog should be sorted with the most valuable items at the top and the least valuable at the bottom. By always working in priority order, the team is able to maximize the value of the product or system being developed.

Roman Pichler, author of *"Agile Product Management with Scrum: Creating Products That Customers Love"*

177

Creating a Product Backlog

1. Create requirements
2. Prioritize Requirements based upon Roadmap and Release Plan
3. Estimate Requirements
4. Update every Sprint – Backlog refinement
5. Consider a requirements hierarchy

178

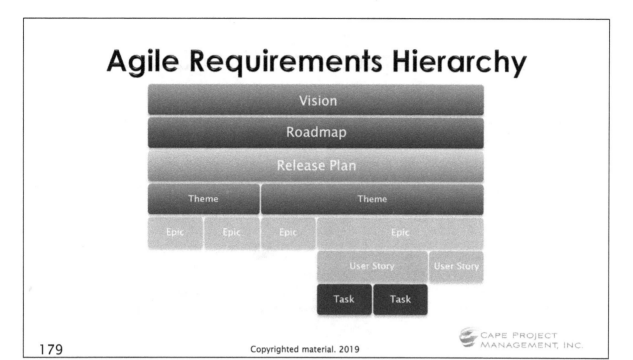

Themes, Epics and User Stories

Themes
▸ Themes are groups of related stories. Often the stories all contribute to a common goal or are related in some obvious way, such as all focusing on a single function.

Epics
▸ Epics resemble themes in the sense that they are made up of multiple stories. As opposed to themes, however, these stories often comprise a complete workflow for a user.

User Stories
▸ A User story is a self-contained unit of work agreed upon by the developers and the stakeholders. Stories are the building blocks of your sprint.

Requirements Considerations

▶ Written requirements
  ◦ can be well thought through, reviewed and edited
  ◦ provide a permanent record
  ◦ are easily shared with groups of people
  ◦ time consuming to produce
  ◦ may be less relevant or superseded over time
  ◦ can be easily misinterpreted
▶ Verbal requirements
  ◦ instantaneous feedback and clarification
  ◦ information-packed exchange
  ◦ easier to clarify and gain common understanding
  ◦ easily adapted to any new information known at the time
  ◦ can spark ideas about problems and opportunities
  ◦ can be vague if they are not validated

Key Principles for Agile Requirements

- ‣ Active user involvement is imperative
- ‣ Agile teams must be empowered to make decisions
- ‣ Requirements emerge and evolve as software is developed
- ‣ Agile requirements are 'barely sufficient'
- ‣ Requirements are developed in small pieces
- ‣ Enough is enough – apply the 80/20 rule
- ‣ Cooperation, collaboration and communication between all team members is essential
- ‣ All requirements as captured in as product backlog items (PBIs)
- ‣ Agile requirements are often written as User Stories

185   Copyrighted material. 2019

User Stories

seek to combine the strengths of written and verbal communication, where possible supported by a picture.

* Kent Beck coined the term user stories in Extreme Programming Explained 1st Edition, 1999

186   Copyrighted material. 2019

Agile Requirements - User Stories

- Agreement between customer and developer to have a conversation.
- A User Story is a very high-level definition of a requirement.
- Contains just enough information to produce a reasonable estimate of the effort to implement it.
- Product Owner writes User Stories on behalf of customer
  - Written in language of business to allow prioritization
  - Customer is primary product visionary

Copyrighted material. 2019 CAPE PROJECT MANAGEMENT, INC.

User Stories have 3 parts

Card *What is the goal of a user*	As a (user role), I want to (goal) so I can (reason) *Example:* *As a registered student, I want to view course details so I can create my schedule*
Conversation *How to achieve the goal using the system?*	Discuss the card with a stakeholder. Just in time analysis (JIT) through conversations. *Example:* *What information is needed to search for a course?* *What information is displayed?*
Confirmation *How to verify if the story is done and complete, and the goal is achieved*	Record what you learn in an acceptance test. *Example:* *Student can access course catalog 24 x 7 hours* *Student cannot choose more than three courses*

http://ronjeffries.com/xprog/articles/expcardconversationconfirmation/

Copyrighted material. 2019 CAPE PROJECT MANAGEMENT, INC.

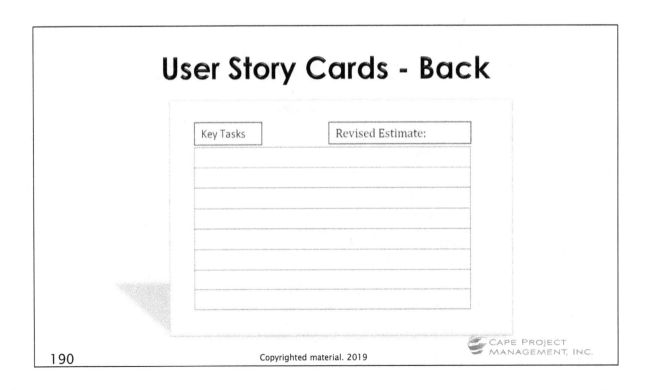

Why use User Stories?

- Keep the focus on expressing business value
- Avoids introducing detail too early that would prevent design options and inappropriately lock developers into one solution
- Avoids the appearance of false completeness and clarity
- Invites negotiation and movement in the backlog
- Leaves the technical functions to the architect, developers, testers, and so on

Note: Certain technical User Stories do not lend themselves to this format

CAPE PROJECT MANAGEMENT, INC.

Requirements vs. User stories

Requirements:

3.4)   The Product needs to have an engine

3.5)   The Product needs to have 4 wheels

     3.5.1) The Product needs to have rubber tires

3.6)   The Product needs to have steering and acceleration

3.7)   The Product needs to have a frame of steel

What are you thinking of?

CAPE PROJECT MANAGEMENT, INC.

Requirements vs. User stories

193

User story:

As a gardener, I want an tool that allows me to mow my lawn faster and easier than with my current hand mower.

The team will have ask additional questions like :

- How big is your lawn ?
- What did you mean by "faster" and "easier?"

Acceptance criteria:

- I want to be able to mow 1 acre in 30 minutes
- I want to sit comfortably.

193

CAPE PROJECT
MANAGEMENT, INC.

Write Stories by Role

- ▸ Define Roles
- ▸ Brainstorm an initial set of user roles
- ▸ Organize the initial set
- ▸ Consolidate roles
- ▸ Refine the roles
- ▸ Prioritize by role

194

CAPE PROJECT
MANAGEMENT, INC.

What to consider when defining roles

▸ Frequency with which user will use software

▸ User's level of expertise with domain

▸ User's general level of proficiency with computers and software

▸ User's level of proficiency with this software

▸ User's general goal for using software

195   Copyrighted material. 2019   CAPE PROJECT MANAGEMENT, INC.

Writing Stories

▸ Good stories are:
  ◦ Independent
  ◦ Negotiable
  ◦ Valuable to users or customers
  ◦ Estimable
  ◦ Small
  ◦ Testable (INVEST)

196   Copyrighted material. 2019   CAPE PROJECT MANAGEMENT, INC.

Independent

- ▸ Stories that depend on other stories are difficult to prioritize and estimate
- ▸ Dependent Story:
  - ◦ As a user, I want to be able to log in and change my password
- ▸ Independent Stories
  - ◦ As a user, I want to be able to log in
  - ◦ As a user, I want the ability to change my password

197   Copyrighted material. 2019   CAPE PROJECT MANAGEMENT, INC.

Negotiable

- ▸ User Stories serve as reminders not contracts
- ▸ The story should convey the problem, not the solution. This way the solution is negotiable.
- ▸ Details need to be fleshed out in conversation

198   Copyrighted material. 2019   CAPE PROJECT MANAGEMENT, INC.

Valuable

- ▸ Both to people using the software and paying for the software
- ▸ Avoid stories valued only by developers (make the benefits to customers/users apparent for these stories)
- ▸ Example
  - ◦ "All connections to the database are through a connection pool" could be rewritten as "Up to 50 users should be able to use the application with a 5-user database license"

Estimable

- ▸ 3 common reasons why a story might not be estimable
- ▸ Not enough information or team lacks domain knowledge
  - ◦ Get details from customer
- ▸ New technology or not enough knowledge in the team
  - ◦ Perform spike to explore technology
- ▸ Story is too big
  - ◦ Split the story into smaller ones

Spikes

- Spikes, an invention of XP, are a special type of User Story used to drive out risk and uncertainty.
- Spikes may be used for basic research to familiarize the team with a new technology or domain.
- They are time-boxed to prevent excess analysis.
- Spikes may be used for estimating features in the next Sprint

Copyrighted material. 2019 CAPE PROJECT MANAGEMENT, INC.

Small

- Small enough to use in planning
- Split Compound or Complex Stories
  - Conversations may reveal multiple stories
  - Split along Create/Replace/Update/Delete (CRUD)
  - Split along data boundaries
  - Use spikes to analyze complexity
- Combine too small stories
  - If a story is too small, it will take more time to define and test than to develop

Copyrighted material. 2019 CAPE PROJECT MANAGEMENT, INC.

Vertical Slices for Splitting

CAPE PROJECT
MANAGEMENT, INC.

Business Driven Approach to Splitting

Pattern	Before	After
CRUD Create / Read / Update / Delete	As a customer, I can manage my account	… sign up for an account … view my account settings … edit my account settings … I cancel my account
Workflow	As a user, I want to use a check-out cart so that I can buy selected items	… enter my home and shipping addresses in checkout … see the shipping costs calculated for my shipping address … get an itemized view of all charges before I submit
Business Rules	As a user, I want to pay by online	… to pay by Mastercard … to pay by Visa … to pay by PayPal … Investigate Bitcoin processing (Spike)
Screens	As a user I want to update my profile	… to update my billing information … to update my contact information … to change my password
Complexity	As a user I can search for products	… I can use a one word search for products … I can use multiple words to search for products … I can search with missplelled words

CAPE PROJECT
MANAGEMENT, INC.

DISCUSSION

How would you split these stories?
As a faculty member I want to search for a student.
As a student I want to pay online.
As An administrator I want to enter free text on screen.

205

Testable

▸ Can't tell if story is "done" without tests
▸ Aim for most tests to be automated
▸ Include Acceptance Criteria as part of the User Story

206

Acceptance Criteria

- Acceptance criteria define the boundaries of a User Story, and are used to confirm when a story is completed and working as intended.
- The tests are written before development
- They are ideally created by the Product Owner
- Does not replace unit tests
- Often written on the back of the User Story card

207
Copyrighted material. 2019

Writing Acceptance Tests

As a student, I want shopping cart functionality to easily pay tuition online.

Acceptance Criteria

- Student information is retained in a database
- Payment can be made via credit card, debit card, or PayPal
- An acknowledgment email is sent to the student after completing the transaction

208
Copyrighted material. 2019

Why use Acceptance Tests?

- ‣ They get the team to think through how a feature or piece of functionality will work from the user's perspective
- ‣ They remove ambiguity from requirements
- ‣ They form the tests that will confirm that a feature or piece of functionality is working and complete.

209

Copyrighted material. 2019

CAPE PROJECT
MANAGEMENT, INC.

GROUP EXERCISE

Exercise 5:
Evaluate Stories

210

Copyrighted material. 2019

CAPE PROJECT
MANAGEMENT, INC.

User Story Examples: LMS Project

Theme 1: Document Management and Editing		Good/Bad
As a Faculty Member, I want...	assignments submitted via the LMS to be searched for direct quotes, so that I can identify students and work with plagiarism.	
As a Faculty Member, I want...	the first release to be in 4 months so that I can use it in the Fall semester	
As a Faculty Member, I want...	to download completed assignments directly to my computer, so that I can view files outside the LMS.	
As a Faculty Member, I want...	to ensure the Helvetica is part of the font set since it is the most readable heading font	
As a Student, I want...	to upload my completed assignments in less than 10 seconds	
As a Student, I want...	to upload content to the LMS as a PDF, so I can protect my content from editing.	
As a Student, I want...	to export the content of a discussion, so that I can view, edit and save in a word processing application on my desktop.	
Theme 2: Assessment & Grading		
As a Faculty Member, I want...	to import exams/assessments and exam questions from external sources (e.g. as MS-Word documents), so that I don't have to reenter them in the LMS.	
As a Faculty Member, I want...	I want to save my grades to f:/grades/instructors/ so that I can review them when I am not online	
As a Faculty Member, I want...	to calculate grades based on weighted averages, so that students always know their standing in the course.	
As a Faculty Member, I want...	to allow individual students to view individual grades, so that students can see their grades per assignment.	
As a Faculty Member, I want...	to export grades as a .xlsx file so that I can read and manipulate them in Excel 2010	
As a Student, I want to...	the option of showing everyone's grades in the class anonymously, so that students can compare their grades with the rest of the class.	
As a Student, I want to...	view all of my grades across all courses, so I do not need to enter each course.	
As a Student, I want to...	I want to be able to provide access to my parents to view my grades	

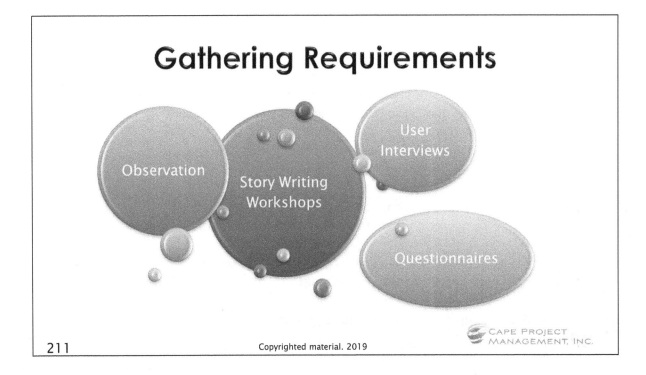

Story-Writing Workshops

- Begin with vision, roadmap and release plan review
- Write as many stories as possible within a timebox – similar to brainstorming
- Involves stakeholders and Scrum Team
- Combine with low-fidelity prototyping or story boarding
- Ask questions that will help identify new stories:
  - What will user likely do next?
  - What mistakes could they make?
  - What could confuse them?
  - What additional information might they need?
- This workshop does not prioritize and estimate the user stories but solely identifies requirements.

Mike Cohn, User Stories Applied

GROUP EXERCISE

Exercise 6:
Story Writing Workshop

213

GROUP EXERCISE

Exercise 7:
Peer Review

214

Priority:

Size:

As a:

I want to:(what)

So that: (why)

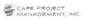
User Story Template

Tasks

User Story Template

When is a User Story Ready?

▸ A story is **clear** if all Scrum team members have a shared understanding of what it means.
▸ An item is **testable** if there is an effective way to determine if the functionality works as expected. Acceptance criteria exists ensure that each story can be tested, typically there are three to five acceptance criteria per User Story.
▸ A story is **feasible** if it can be completed in one Sprint, according to the definition of done.
▸ **Ready** stories are the output of the product backlog refinement work.

215

Copyrighted material. 2019

CAPE PROJECT
MANAGEMENT, INC.

Example Definition of "Ready"

▸ Story meets the criteria of INVEST
▸ Story traceable to source document (where appropriate)
▸ Acceptance criteria defined
▸ Size estimated by delivery team
▸ User experience included (where appropriate)
▸ Performance criteria identified (where appropriate)
▸ Person who will accept the User Story is identified
▸ Team has a good idea about how to demo the User Story

216

Copyrighted material. 2019

CAPE PROJECT
MANAGEMENT, INC.

Additional Agile Requirements Techniques

Personas
Technical Requirements
Wireframes & Story boards
Agile Use Cases

Personas

- ‣ Archetypal users of an application
- ‣ Fictitious but based upon knowledge of real users
- ‣ Help guide the functionality and design
- ‣ More accurate user stories can be written using personas

- ‣ As a user, I want to add a calendar entry
  - ◦ As an admin, I want to create a calendar entry for an executive
  - ◦ As an executive, I want to create a calendar entry for myself

Persona Components

- Personal profile
- Experience
- Personal goals
- Professional goals

Copyrighted material. 2019

Persona Example

- Jim is 50 years old and works as a mechanic with a company offering road service to customers when their car breaks down. He has worked in the job for the past 10 years and knows it well. Many of the younger mechanics ask Jim for advice. He always knows the answer to tricky mechanical problems.
- He is getting a new computer installed in his van. He doesn't own a computer, and he is a little intimidated by this type of technology.
- He is very nervous that he is going to look stupid if he can't figure it out.

What should you consider when building this system?

Copyrighted material. 2019

Activity: Create an Extreme Persona

Directions:

1. Pick a role from your case study. Create an Extreme Persona for supporting the requirements process.
2. Create a profile below.
3. Be prepared to share your answers with the class.

Personal Profile	

Activity

Exercise 8:
Create an extreme persona
Select a role from your case study

221   Copyrighted material. 2019   CAPE PROJECT
MANAGEMENT, INC.

Technical Requirements

▸ Written by development team, architect, tech lead
▸ Don't have to be written as User Stories
▸ Often part of the Definition of Done
▸ Non-Functional Requirements (NFRs) should be part of the Acceptance Criteria

222   Copyrighted material. 2019   CAPE PROJECT
MANAGEMENT, INC.

Technical Requirements in DoD

- All code must be peer reviewed within 4 hours of check-in.
- If a change is made to the web services interface, the change must be documented on the official web services api wiki page.
- All code must have automated testing that is consistent with the "Automated Testing Guidelines"

223   Copyrighted material. 2019   CAPE PROJECT MANAGEMENT, INC.

NFRs in Acceptance Criteria

Requirement type	Example
Performance	• Any interaction between the user and the system should not exceed 2 seconds. • The system should receive updated student information every 15 minutes.
Security	• Only direct managers can see personnel records of staff • Only students and bursar's office can see payment information
Cultural & Political	• The system should be able to distinguish between United States and European currency • The system shall comply with industry privacy standards.

224   Copyrighted material. 2019   CAPE PROJECT MANAGEMENT, INC.

Prioritizing Technical Requirements

▸ Projects have to balance delivering features along with doing all the important behind-the-scenes work.

▸ Leaving non-functional development until very late in the project has two major problems:

1. It costs more
2. It creates project risks that can lead to project problems

225

Wireframes

▸ "User Stories seek to combine the strengths of written and verbal communication, where possible supported by a **picture**."

▸ Low-fidelity (prototype)

▸ Black and white

▸ Combined to create a story board – sequence of screens

▸ Iteratively improved

▸ Validates design and understanding of user stories

226

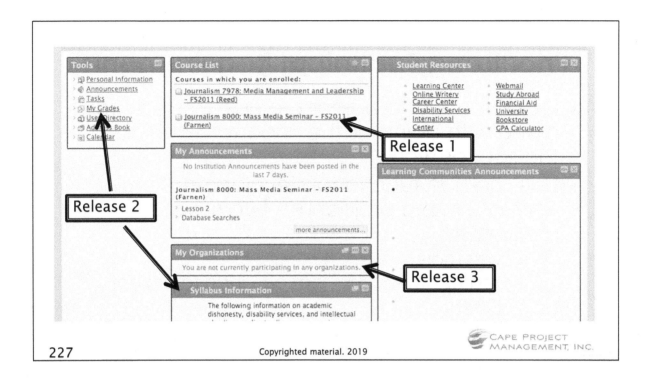

CAPE PROJECT
MANAGEMENT, INC.

Use Cases versus User Story

A Use Case is:	A User Story is:
▸ the specification of a set of actions	▸ a simple, clear, brief description
▸ performed by a system	▸ expressing a user's goal for using the system under development
▸ yields an observable result of value for one or more actors of the system.	▸ to deliver business value

▪Both methods are focusing on users and values to the users
▪Each has its own challenges
▪Use cases are often used for new products and user stories for incremental releases

CAPE PROJECT
MANAGEMENT, INC.

Agile Use Cases

- Write just enough content to plan the needed horizon
  - Project and release planning-> use briefs.
  - Sprint planning-> Full use case and extension handling.
- Just barely beat the programmers to the extension handling decisions
- Write just enough content for the team to understand.
- Show the Use Cases to stakeholders for feedback

Use Case Briefs

- Write briefs to estimate & plan project.

Actor	Goal	Brief Description
Student	Register for Courses On-line	Student searches for course by major, identifies available timeslots, registers and receives confirmation

- Write full use cases just-in-time

Full Use Case

Course Enrollment
1. Student requests to create a schedule.
2. The system prepares a blank schedule form.
3. The system gets available courses from the Course Catalog System.
4. Student selects up to 4 primary and 2 alternate course offerings.
5. For each course, the system verifies that the Student has the necessary prerequisites, adds the Student to the course, marking Student as "enrolled" for that course in the schedule.
6. The Student indicates the schedule is complete, the system saves it.

Extensions:
1a. Student already has a schedule: System brings up the current version of the Student's schedule for editing instead of creating a new one.
1b. Current semester is closed and next semester is not yet open: System lets Student look at existing schedules, but not create new ones.
3a. Course Catalog System does not respond: The system notifies the Student and the use case ends.
5a. Course full or Student has not fulfilled all prerequisites: System disables selection of that course and notifies the Student

---

Guidelines for Agile Requirements

- ▸ Start with themes or epics
- ▸ Create user stories that meet the criteria of INVEST
- ▸ Include user roles in stories rather than saying "user"
- ▸ Don't rely solely on stories if they can be better expressed in other ways
- ▸ Size your story appropriately for the time frame it may be implemented in
- ▸ Ensure all completed stories meet a definition of "Done"

Prioritizing in Agile

Module 3

Copyrighted material. 2019

CAPE PROJECT MANAGEMENT, INC.

Prioritize items in a backlog

▸ The Product Owner prioritizes the product backlog items
▸ The backlog is prioritized so that the most valuable items have the highest priorities
▸ Prioritization by Release translates to the Product Roadmap

PRIORITY

1.
2.
3.

Copyrighted material. 2019

CAPE PROJECT MANAGEMENT, INC.

Agile Triangle

Value
- Meets or exceeds customer value expectations
- Value "chunks" are delivered in time-boxed releases

Quality
- Today's quality: Is the product reliable?
- Tomorrow's quality: Is the product adaptable to change?

Constraints
- Scope: all planned major value-generating capabilities are delivered.
- Cost: actual costs are within agreed to limits
- Schedule: actual schedule is within agreed to limits

235

Focus on Value

The Traditional Iron Triangle

The Agile Triangle

236

Quality Defined

▸ Intrinsic Quality
  ◦ All of the qualities that were built into the product: suitability, durability, reliability, uniformity, maintainability.

▸ Extrinsic Quality
  ◦ Perceived quality
  ◦ Value to the customer

Kelada, Joseph, *Integrating Reengineering with Total Quality*

237   Copyrighted material. 2019

Determining Value
Quantitative versus Qualitative

Quantitative Techniques
▸ Return on investment (ROI)
▸ Net present value (NPV)
▸ Internal rate of return (IRR)
▸ Payback Period
Qualitative Techniques
▸ Cumulative voting (the money game)
▸ Kano analysis
▸ Risk-based prioritization
▸ Weight Shortest Job First (WSJF)
▸ MoSCoW prioritization

238   Copyrighted material. 2019

Cumulative Voting

- ‣ Hundred dollar method
- ‣ Give each stakeholder $100 in play money and they can "spend" it the requirements they want the most
- ‣ Can use points, stickers, etc.

239

Kano Analysis

Need	Definition
Exciters/Delighters	Exceeds customer needs, and a "nice to have." Contributes 100% to positive customer satisfaction.
Performance/Linear	Competitive requirements that the customer "wants", typically an improvement over current system.
Basic/Baseline	Meets minimum requirements and is a "must have." If these features don't exist, the customer is dissatisfied.
Indifferent	Least important to the customer. They will likely return little or no business value.

240

Kano Analysis, Graphical

"Kano model showing transition over time" by Craig W Brown – Own work. Licensed under CC BY–SA 3.0 via Wikimedia Commons – Source:
http://commons.wikimedia.org/wiki/File:Kano_model_showing_transition_over_time.png#/media/File:Kano_model_showing_transition_over_time.png

241   Copyrighted material. 2019   CAPE PROJECT MANAGEMENT, INC.

Risk-based Prioritization

- Complete high-value, high-risk stories first
- Complete high-value, low-risk stories next
- Complete lower-value, low-risk stories next
- Avoid low-value, high-risk stories

242   Copyrighted material. 2019   CAPE PROJECT MANAGEMENT, INC.

Weighted Shortest Job First (WSJF)

▸ "Low Hanging Fruit" approach
▸ Assign a value to each story and divide that that by the length by the job size (points) determine a relative ranking.

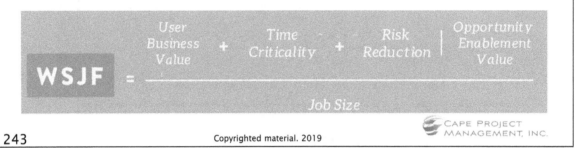

$$WSJF = \frac{User\ Business\ Value + Time\ Criticality + Risk\ Reduction\ |\ Opportunity\ Enablement\ Value}{Job\ Size}$$

243

CAPE PROJECT
MANAGEMENT, INC.

MoSCoW Prioritization

Acronym	Description
M – MUST	Describes a requirement that must be satisfied in the final solution for the solution to be considered a success.
S – SHOULD	Represents a high-priority item that should be included in the solution if it is possible. This is often a critical requirement but one which can be satisfied in other ways if strictly necessary.
C – COULD	Describes a requirement which is considered desirable but not necessary. This will be included if time and resources permit.
W – WON'T	Represents a requirement that stakeholders have agreed will not be implemented in a given release, but may be considered for the future.

244

CAPE PROJECT
MANAGEMENT, INC.

GROUP EXERCISE

Exercise 9:
Prioritize User Stories

245

CAPE PROJECT
MANAGEMENT, INC.

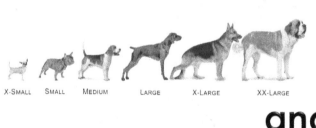

X-SMALL   SMALL   MEDIUM   LARGE   X-LARGE   XX-LARGE

Agile Sizing
and Estimating
Module 4

246

CAPE PROJECT
MANAGEMENT, INC.

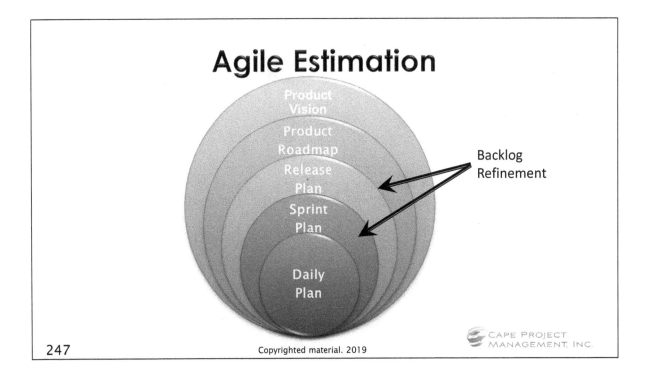

247

Reviewing Stories in Backlog Refinement

Product Owner
- Orders and reviews backlog
- Makes priority adjustments based on feedback from delivery team
- Ensures that higher priority items have more detail

Delivery Team
- Asks questions
- Understands the objective, not just the desired features
  - Key to flexibility and risk management
- Breaks large stories (Epics) into smaller stories
- Estimates Story Sizes

248

Agile Sizing and Estimating

- Assumes all traditional estimates are inaccurate, essentially we are guessing
- Focuses on rapid/order of magnitude estimating
- There are many Agile Estimating Tools and Techniques
- Occurs during backlog refinement and Sprint planning

CAPE PROJECT MANAGEMENT, INC.

Traditional Estimating

Cone of Uncertainty: The amount of possible error in a software project estimate, which is very large in the early stages of a project and shrinks dramatically as the project nears completion

~ Steve McConnell, Software Estimation: Demystifying the Black Art

Chart x-axis: Feasibility, Concept of Operation, Requirements Spec, Product Design Spec, Detail Design Spec, Accepted Software

Legend: Minimum, Maximum

CAPE PROJECT MANAGEMENT, INC.

Agile Estimating Techniques

- Swimlane Sizing
- Story points
- Planning poker
- Fibonacci Sequence

251

CAPE PROJECT MANAGEMENT, INC.

Relative Estimating using Swim lanes

- Order each user story from easiest to hardest
- Group similar size stories together
- Leave a column for Epics
- Label using Story Points

http://theagilepirate.net/archives/109

252

CAPE PROJECT MANAGEMENT, INC.

Story Points

- The "bigness" of a task
- Influenced by:
  - How hard it is
  - How much of it there is
- Relative values are what is important:
  - A login screen is a 2.
  - A search feature is an 8.
- Points are unit-less

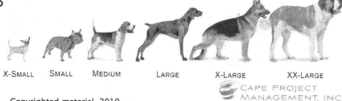

X-Small   Small   Medium   Large   X-Large   XX-Large

253

CAPE PROJECT
MANAGEMENT, INC.

Benchmarking

| Select a benchmark story or stories | Estimate each additional story by comparing it to the benchmark | If a User Story is bigger than an iteration or difficult to size use a very large number |

If multiple teams are working on the same backlog, they need the same benchmarks.

254

CAPE PROJECT
MANAGEMENT, INC.

Planning Poker

1. Each team member is given a deck of cards
2. Product-Owner reads a story
3. The story is briefly discussed, questions answered etc.
4. Each team member secretly selects a card that is his or her estimate
5. Cards are presented to the group at the same time
6. Differences and outliers are discussed
7. Re-estimate until estimates converge

255

CAPE PROJECT MANAGEMENT, INC.

Avoid "Anchoring"

- Anchoring is a where the estimates of individuals are biased based on irrelevant information or strong personalities
- As a result, members will subconsciously use the given estimate as an anchor.
- To avoid this, the Scrum Master should instruct the team to estimate for themselves.
- Team members should reveal at the same time.

256

CAPE PROJECT MANAGEMENT, INC.

Fibonacci Sequence

- ‣ 0 1 1 2 3 5 8 13 21 34 55...
- ‣ Often aligned with T-shirt sizes: XS,S,M,L,XL
- ‣ Provides more flexibility for unknown larger stories
- ‣ Limit the largest number
- ‣ Use cards to estimate
  - ◦ Similar to planning poker

CAPE PROJECT MANAGEMENT, INC.

GROUP EXERCISE

Exercise 10: Estimate User Stories

 CAPE PROJECT MANAGEMENT, INC.

Sprint Planning

Sprint Backlog

CAPE PROJECT MANAGEMENT, INC.

Sprint Planning

▸ The Development Team works with the Product owner to select those items that meet the Sprint Goal and will fit in a Sprint
▸ Based upon a refined Product Backlog
  ◦ Prioritized Stories
  ◦ Estimated Stories
▸ Sprint Backlog is created based upon story size, priority and velocity
▸ The Sprint Backlog is emergent and will evolve during the Sprint to meet the Sprint goal

CAPE PROJECT MANAGEMENT, INC.

Reviewing Stories

▸ Product Owner
  ◦ Explain the Sprint objective
  ◦ Present the User Stories which will meet the objective
  ◦ Make priority adjustments based on feedback from delivery team
▸ Delivery Team
  ◦ Ask Questions
  ◦ Understand the objective, not just the desired features
  ◦ Collaborates with the Product Owner to create the Sprint Goal

261

CAPE PROJECT
MANAGEMENT, INC.

The Commitment (Forecast)

▸ By the end of the Sprint Planning, the Development Team should be able to explain to the Product Owner and Scrum Master how it intends to work as a self-organizing team to accomplish the Sprint Goal and create the anticipated Increment. ~Scrum Guide
▸ Drive agreement with a fist of five
  • This is the best idea possible
  • The only thing wrong with this idea is that it wasn't mine
  • I can support this idea
  • I'm uneasy about this and think we need to talk it out some more
  • Let's continue discussing this idea in the parking lot

262

CAPE PROJECT
MANAGEMENT, INC.

Daily Planning

Tasks

263

CAPE PROJECT
MANAGEMENT, INC.

Define Tasks

▸ Through conversation among the team, define tasks
  ◦ Don't make task too granular (don't do 10 minute tasks)
  ◦ Don't make task too large (1 sprint length)
▸ Team members sign up for tasks, they are not assigned
▸ Any team member can add, delete, or change tasks, they often emerge during the Sprint

264

CAPE PROJECT
MANAGEMENT, INC.

Create User Story Tasks

User Story	Tasks
As a student, I want to be able to log in to the system	Design the...
	Meet with customer
	Design the UI
	Code and Unit Test the..
	Automate Tests...
As a faculty member, I want to update my contact information	Copy admin profile
	Design solution to..
	Validate Workflow
	Code the..
	Automate tests..

265

CAPE PROJECT
MANAGEMENT, INC.

Avoid Mini-Waterfall

266

CAPE PROJECT
MANAGEMENT, INC.

Team Swarm (or Swarming)

- ‣ Working on one or more stories until they are done
- ‣ Each story has a "TeamLet"
- ‣ Each TeamLet has:
  - ◦ A **Coordinator** who is in charge of the story and stays with it until it is complete
  - ◦ A **Swarmer(s)** brings their expertise to the story. A Swarmer may be on multiple TeamLets.

CAPE PROJECT MANAGEMENT, INC.

Agile Controls

Module 10

CAPE PROJECT MANAGEMENT, INC.

Agile Controls

- ▸ Quality Control
- ▸ Measuring Success
- ▸ Risk Management

Copyrighted material. 2019 CAPE PROJECT MANAGEMENT, INC.

Agile Quality Assurance & Control

- ▸ Product Owner/Customer in the Team
  - ◦ Software that meets the Product Owner's intent
  - ◦ Product Owner is the single owner of quality and becomes part of the team and guides development.
- ▸ Releasable Software in every Timebox, which:
  - ◦ Meets the Product Owner's expectations
  - ◦ Adheres to a Definition of Done
  - ◦ Has to best design for the currently implemented features (via refactoring)
  - ◦ Is easily maintainable (via refactoring)
  - ◦ Has been tested to the satisfaction of the team and relevant stakeholders
  - ◦ Is value-driven
- ▸ Iterative and Continuous Product Reviews
  - ◦ Results are documented and incorporated into backlog
  - ◦ Defects are managed as backlog items
  - ◦ Technical debt is more prevalent on Agile teams
- ▸ Definition of Done is the primary Quality Control tool

Copyrighted material. 2019 CAPE PROJECT MANAGEMENT, INC.

The Definition of Done?

"The Definition of Done (DoD) as a tool for bringing transparency to the work a Scrum Team is performing. It is related more to the quality of a product, rather than its functionality." ~Scrum Guide

- Defined by Product Owner and Team and updated every Sprint
- Considerations
  - Quality Metrics
  - Coding standards
  - Test coverage
  - Integration testing
  - Documented (just *enough*)
- Risks of unclear definition
  - Inaccurate Velocity
  - Technical debt
- 0/100% Rule

https://www.scrum.org/Resources/Scrum-Glossary/Definition-of-Done

271

CAPE PROJECT
MANAGEMENT, INC.

Good Enough Artifacts

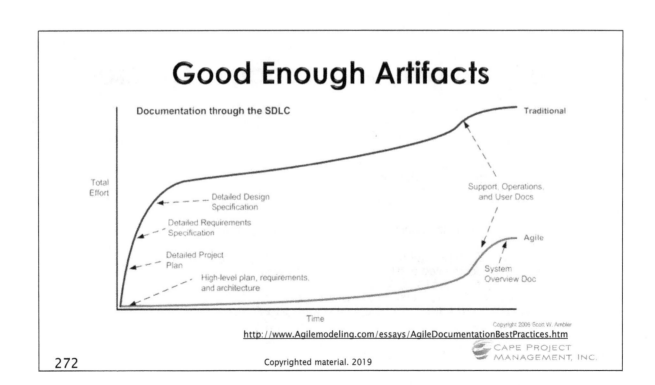

Documentation through the SDLC

Total Effort

Traditional

Detailed Design Specification

Detailed Requirements Specification

Detailed Project Plan

High-level plan, requirements, and architecture

Support, Operations, and User Docs

Agile

System Overview Doc

Time

Copyright 2006 Scott W. Ambler

http://www.Agilemodeling.com/essays/AgileDocumentationBestPractices.htm

272

CAPE PROJECT
MANAGEMENT, INC.

Definition of Done

Example
- All code peer reviewed
- Compliant with coding standards
- Static testing with 0 errors and 0 warnings
- Dynamic testing – no memory leaks
- All code checked in to Subversion prod branch
- 80% code coverage – unit testing
- Zero known bugs
- Acceptance tests verified by QA on clean system
- Acceptance tests verified by Product Owner or proxy

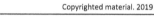

www.threebeacons.com white paper "The Three Beacons of Software Project Success"

273

CAPE PROJECT
MANAGEMENT, INC.

GROUP EXERCISE

Exercise 11: Define Done

274

CAPE PROJECT
MANAGEMENT, INC.

Activity: Definition on Done

Directions:
1. Return to your groups that developed the User Stories for the Case Study
2. Define done using the suggestions on the slides
3. Make sure some form of acceptance testing included
4. List the suggestions as if you would be posting this sheet on a war room wall

Definition of Done:

The Evolution of a User Story

Exploratory Testing

- Unscripted testing where testers generally explore the application's functionality without restraint
- Encourage testers to plan as they test and to use information gathered during testing to affect the actual way testing is performed
- Often occurs after the iteration in the period between "done" and "done, done." Also called a Hardening Iteration
- Always performed in conjunction with traditional testing

276

CAPE PROJECT MANAGEMENT, INC.

Technical Debt

- Development decisions made in the short term which cause more work in the long-term
- Not necessarily apparent to the user
- Difficult to measure because the code meets test cases and is not a defect
- Major challenge of Agile
- The higher the technical debt means the lower the intrinsic quality of the product
- Product Owner can work with the Development Team to reduce technical debt by improving the Definition of Done.

277

CAPE PROJECT MANAGEMENT, INC.

Measuring Success in Agile

Business Outcomes (Value)	Time to Market (Lead Time)	Ability to Innovate (Quality)
• Revenue per Employee • Employee Satisfaction • Customer Satisfaction	• Release Frequency • Release Stabilization • Cycle Time	• Product Cost Ratio • Installed Version Index • Usage Index • Innovation Rate • Defects

http://www.ebmgt.org/portals/agilitypath/Documents/EBMgt_Guide_v1_CWT.pdf

278

CAPE PROJECT MANAGEMENT, INC.

Current Value Metrics

Revenue per Employee	Gross Revenue / #employees
Product Cost Ratio	All expenses in the organization that develops, sustains, provides services, markets, sells, and administers the product or system.
Employee Satisfaction	Engaged employees that know how to maintain, sustain and enhance the software systems and products are one of the most significant assets of an organization.
Customer Satisfaction	Sound management, solid software, and creative, fulfilled employees.

279

CAPE PROJECT MANAGEMENT, INC.

Time to Market Metrics

Release Frequency	The time needed to satisfy the customer with new, competitive products.
Release Stabilization	The impact of poor development practices and underlying design and code base. Stabilization is a drag on competition that grows with time.
Cycle Time	The time (including stabilization) to satisfy a key set of customers or to respond to a market opportunity competitively.

280

CAPE PROJECT MANAGEMENT, INC.

Ability to Innovate Metrics

Installed Version Index	The difficulty customers face installing a new release .The relatively low value of new releases, or even the # of customers that are evaluating alternatives.
Usage Index	Determines a product that is burdensome and difficult to use and excess software that must be sustained even though it is rarely used.
Innovation Rate	Growth of technical debt caused by poorly designed and developed software. Budget is progressively consumed keeping the old software alive.
Defects	Measures increasingly poor quality software, leading to greater resource and budget to maintain it and potential loss of customers.

CAPE PROJECT MANAGEMENT, INC.

281

Other KPIs for Agile

‣ Team Velocity – the consistency of the team's estimates from iteration to iteration.
‣ Actual Stories Completed vs. Committed Stories – the team's ability to understand and predict its capabilities.
‣ Technical Debt Management – the known problems and issues delivered at the end of the Sprint.
‣ Quality Delivered to Customers –best measured by surveying the customers and stakeholders.
‣ Team Enthusiasm –it is a major component for a successful Agile team. Also known as "happiness metric"
‣ Retrospective Process Improvement – the Team's ability to revise its development process to make itself more effective and enjoyable for the next iteration.

http://pragmaticmarketing.com/resources/9-Scrum-metrics-to-keep-your-team-on-track

CAPE PROJECT MANAGEMENT, INC.

282

Risk Management in Agile

‣ Agile mitigates the most commons project risks:
- ◦ Intrinsic Schedule Flaw
- ◦ Specification Breakdown
- ◦ Scope Creep
- ◦ Personnel Loss
- ◦ Productivity Variance

‣ Risk management in Agile is "organic", since risk is addressed naturally as part of the project lifecycle.

CAPE PROJECT
MANAGEMENT, INC.

Do You Recognize These Risks?

Risk	Agile Mitigation
Misunderstanding of the requirements	Short delivery cycles with continuous feedback
Lack of management commitment and support	Stakeholder involvement throughout
Lack of adequate user involvement	Users actively engaged as a team member
Failure to gain user commitment	User creates the requirements
Failure to manage end user expectation	Prioritization by business value
Changes to requirements	Embrace change
Lack of an effective project management methodology	Repeatable lightweight methodologies

CAPE PROJECT
MANAGEMENT, INC.

Implementing Agile

Module 11

CAPE PROJECT
MANAGEMENT, INC.

Start with the Basics

		PROCESS AGREEMENTS
1.	COMMON UNDERSTANDING OF SCRUM ROLES	
2.	TEAM ARRANGEMENTS	
3.	INITIAL PRODUCT VISIONING	PRODUCT VISIONING
4.	USER PERSONAS, USER/MARKET INSIGHTS	
5.	STORY MAPPING	
6.	INITIAL RELEASE PLANNING: MVP, NEXT RELEASES	RELEASE PLANNING
7.	DEFINING DONE	
8.	USER STORY WRITING WORKSHOPS (MINIMUM: PRODUCT BACKLOG FOR THE 1ST SPRINT)	
9.	BACKLOG REFINEMENT	SPRINTING
10.	SPRINT PLANNING	

CAPE PROJECT
MANAGEMENT, INC.

Scrum is "Easy"

- Minimal process overhead
- Less bureaucracy
- Less documentation
- Less surprises

Copyrighted material. 2019

Scrum is Hard

- Change in processes
- Change in bureaucracy
- Change in documentation standards
- Different kinds of surprises

"When you're finished changing, you're finished."
~ Benjamin Franklin

Copyrighted material. 2019

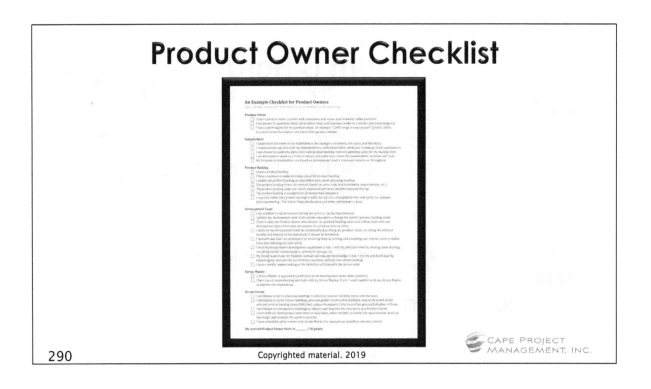

An Example Checklist for Product Owners

Lare Lekman | Revised in November 2013 | productownerchecklist.org

Product Vision
- [ ] I have a product vision (created with customers, end users, and investors, when possible)
- [ ] I can answer to questions about the product vision and business model in a concise and motivating way
- [ ] I have a short tagline for the product vision, for example "1,000 songs in your pocket" (iPod in 2001), to communicate the essence and value of the product release.

Stakeholders
- [ ] I understand the needs of my stakeholders (for example customers, end users, and investors)
- [ ] I communicate regularly with my stakeholders to understand their needs and to manage their expectations
- [ ] I can answer to questions about how each product backlog item will generate value for the stakeholders
- [ ] I am motivated to work as a Product Owner, and make sure I have the stakeholders' mandate and trust
- [ ] My forecasts to stakeholders are based on development team's measured velocity or throughput

Product Backlog
- [ ] I have a product backlog
- [ ] I have a mandate to make decisions about the product backlog
- [ ] I update the product backlog at least before each sprint planning meeting
- [ ] The product backlog items are ordered (based on value, risk, work estimates, dependencies, etc.)
- [ ] The product backlog items are clearly expressed and more detailed towards the top
- [ ] The product backlog is accessible to all scrum team members
- [ ] I regularly refine the product backlog to make the top of it actionable for the next sprint (or release) planning meeting. The Scrum Team decides how and when refinement is done.

Development Team
- [ ] I am available to my developers during the sprint to clarify requirements
- [ ] I protect my development team from anyone who tries to change the sprint's product backlog items
- [ ] There is only one Product Owner who chooses the product backlog items and refines them with the development team. Otherwise, developers do not know who to listen.
- [ ] I motivate my development team by occasionally describing my product vision, including the planned benefits and impacts of the next product release or increment.
- [ ] I motivate and train my developers by involving them in writing and analyzing user stories, when possible (thus also reducing my own work).
- [ ] I trust my Scrum team's development capabilities. If not, I will try and build trust by offering them training, recruiting, better communication, personnel changes, etc.
- [ ] My Scrum team trusts my business domain and end user knowledge. If not, I will try and build trust by improving my own and the Scrum team's business and end user understanding.
- [ ] I have a similar understanding of the Definition of Done with the Scrum team

Scrum Master
- [ ] A Scrum Master is appointed (preferably by the development team, when possible)
- [ ] I have a good understanding and trust with my Scrum Master. If not, I work together with my Scrum Master to improve our cooperation.

Scrum Events
- [ ] I participate in sprint planning meetings to select the product backlog items with the team
- [ ] I participate in sprint review meetings, give and gather constructive feedback, and verify which of the selected product backlog items fulfill their unique Acceptance Criteria and the general Definition of Done.
- [ ] I participate in retrospective meetings to observe and improve my own work as a Product Owner
- [ ] I work with my development team even on daily basis, when needed, to clarify the requirements, work on the design, and optimize the sprint's outcome.
- [ ] I have scheduled sprint events with Scrum Master (for example as repetitive calendar events)

My current Product Owner Score is _____ / 30 points

Preparing for PSPO I or CAPe-PO Exam

- Use our 320 question Practice Exam for up to 90 days
- 80 Questions in one hour
- You can stop and start as much as you want
- Review the Scrum Guide
  - www.scrumguides.org
- Keep taking it until you get 95%
- The actual exam requires 85% (PSPO I) 80% (CAPe-PO)

Login instructions will be delivered via email

291 Copyrighted material. 2019

292 Copyrighted material. 2019

GROUP EXERCISE

Day 2 Review
Agile Jeopardy
http://bit.ly/ScrumGames

293

CAPE PROJECT
MANAGEMENT, INC.

Thank-You!

dan@CapeProjectManagement.com

Twitter: @scrumdan

294

CAPE PROJECT
MANAGEMENT, INC.

User Story References

1. Ralph, Paul (2015). "The Sensemaking-coevolution-implementation theory of software design". Science of Computer Programming. 101: 21–41. arXiv:1302.4061. doi:10.1016/j.scico.2014.11.007.

2. "Origin of story card is a promise for a conversation : Alistair.Cockburn.us". alistair.cockburn.us. Retrieved 2017-08-16.

3. Beck, Kent (1999). "Embracing change with extreme programming". IEEE Computer. 32 (10): 70–77.

4. Ron Jeffries (August 30, 2001). "Essential XP: Card, Conversation, Confirmation".

5. https://www.agilealliance.org/glossary/role-feature/

6. Mishkin Berteig (2014-03-06). "User Stories and Story Splitting". Agile Advice. Retrieved 2017-02-23.

7. AntonyMarcano (2011-03-24). "Old Favourite: Feature Injection User Stories on a Business Value Theme". Antonymarcano.com. Retrieved 2017-02-23.

8. Weldemichael, Weldemichael. "User Story Template Advantages". Mountaingoatsoftware.com. Retrieved 2017-02-23.

9. "10 Tips for Writing Good User Stories". Romanpichler.com. Retrieved 2017-02-23.

10. Cowan, Alexander. "Your Best Agile User Story". Cowan+. Retrieved 29 April 2016.

11. Cohn, Mike. "User Stories". Mountain Goat Software. Retrieved 27 April2016.

12. Ralph, Paul; Mohanani, Rahul. "Is Requirements Engineering Inherently Counterproductive?". IEEE. doi:10.1109/TwinPeaks.2015.12.

13. "Limitations of user stories". Ferolen.com. April 15, 2008.

14. Patton, Jeff. "The new user story backlog is a map". Retrieved 17 May 2017.

15. Pichler, Roman. "10 Tips for Writing Good User Stories". Retrieved 29 July2014.

16. Cohn, Mike. "User Stories, Epics and Themes". Mountaingoatsoftware.com. Retrieved 26 September 2017.

17. Cockburn, Alistair. "Walking Skeleton". Retrieved 4 March 2013.

18. "Story Mapping". Agile Alliance. Retrieved 1 May 2016.

19. Cohn, Mike. "Project Advantages of User Stories as Requirements". Mountaingoatsoftware.com. Retrieved 26 September 2017.

20. Martin Fowler (18 August 2003). "UseCasesAndStories". Retrieved 26 September 2017.

CAPE PROJECT MANAGEMENT, INC.

Appendix

WHAT IS A USER STORY?

A user story is an agile project management tool used to define product or system functionality and the associated benefit of the functionality. In an Agile environment, projects are commonly comprised of a large number of user stories representing various levels of system/product user. The user story describes the type of system/product user, what functionality they want, and why they want it (or why it's beneficial). The format of a user story is:

As a *<type of user>*, I want to *<feature/function>* so that *<reason/benefit>*.

The purpose of the user story is to encourage collaboration among the project team for each defined function of the system or product being developed. Agile project management places emphasis on collaboration rather than formal documentation. Because of this, each user story created by the team represents an opportunity for the team to collaborate, decide which user stories will be worked on in the next Sprint, further define the functionality (during Sprint planning), and accomplish the work.

While user stories represent a simplified approach to defining functionality, the challenge for the project team is developing user stories with the appropriate level of detail.

THE CHARACTERISTICS OF A USER STORY

All user stories should be developed with the expectation that once completed, the functionality defined in the user story will add value to the final product. If it does not add value to the finished product then it should be avoided.

Finding the appropriate level of detail for user stories is often a challenge for the team. User stories should be general enough to provide a description of the functionality and the benefit while also allowing for innovation and creativity for developing a solution. They should not be so detailed as to lock the team into only one way of accomplishing the solution.

In the creation of their user stories, many agile practitioners subscribe to the INVEST acronym created by Bill Wake which states that user stories should be:

Independent – user stories should not be sequential or locked into a specific order. The team should be able to develop the user stories in any sequence.

Negotiable – user stories should be flexible and without too much detail. Details will be added later through team collaboration.

Valuable – the user stories should add value to the final product.

Estimable – the team must be able to use the user stories to estimate/approximate work.

Small – large or vague user stories are difficult to estimate. User stories should be able to be designed, built, and tested within a single Sprint.

Testable – the user story should be able to be tested with some type of acceptance criteria or other test (even if it has not yet been defined)

Acceptance criteria, while not formally a part of the user story format, is a crucial component of user stories. As user stories evolve toward Sprint planning, the team should collaboratively discuss the acceptance criteria for satisfying each user story. Acceptance criteria are used by the team to understand when the intent of the user story has been met. Additionally, acceptance criteria are often used by the product/system testers to develop the acceptance tests for the user story.

Acceptance tests are developed to test the functionality of each user story. While an acceptance criteria ensures that a certain functionality is included in a Sprint, an acceptance test ensures that functionality performs as expected.

WHAT TO AVOID WHEN WRITING USER STORIES

User stories provide an effective tool to encourage communication and collaboration among the team. However, there are several common mistakes that teams make when developing their user stories which often reduce their effectiveness. Some of these mistakes include:

Too much detail – user stories should be broad enough to allow for flexibility and a collaborative effort to further define the user story during Sprint planning when the team agrees to incorporate it into the next Sprint. User stories with too much detail may lock the team into only one way to develop a solution which discourages innovation and creativity.

Lack of acceptance criteria – as user stories evolve, the team must discuss and capture acceptance criteria. Without acceptance criteria, the team will have no ability of knowing when they've satisfied the user story. Additionally, a lack of acceptance criteria will result in a lack of acceptance testing which hampers the team's ability to ensure functionality of the product performs as expected.

EXAMPLES OF USER STORIES: GOOD AND BAD

Below are examples of user stories which include too much detail, not enough detail, and an appropriate amount of detail.

Too Much Detail:
As an end user, I want the ability to access the human resource database to generate a staffing report with employee names, dates of birth, social security numbers, addresses, and telephone numbers so that I can periodically update the company's staffing contact list.

Note that the above example goes into listing details about what the report should include. Including these items in the user story may prevent or discourage the team from including other important content in reports that will be built. This level of detail should be defined later during Sprint planning.

Too Broad:
As an end user, I want access to the human resource database so that I can periodically update the company's staffing contact list.

Note that the above example mentions nothing about the ability to generate reports from the human resource database. Only access to the database is mentioned. By leaving out the key information about generating a report, the team might overlook this important functionality and only grant access to the database when the Sprint is performed.

Appropriate Level of Detail:

As an end user, I want to access the human resource database to generate reports so that I can periodically update the company's staffing contact list.

The above example ensures that when Sprint planning begins, the team can plan for both access and report generating while further defining what information the reports will consist of.

USER STORY WITH ACCEPTANCE CRITERIA AND ACCEPTANCE TESTING

Below is an example of a single user story with both the acceptance criteria and acceptance testing information included.

User Story:

As an end user, I want to access the human resource database to generate reports so that I can periodically update the company's staffing contact list.

Acceptance Criteria:

- Ability to gain access to human resource database
- Ability to generate a report which includes
  - o Employee names
  - o Dates of birth
  - o Social security numbers
  - o Addresses
  - o Telephone numbers
- Ability to use report data to update staffing contact list

Acceptance Testing:

- Database is accessible internally but not from outside company firewall
- MS Access report can be generated from database based on query inputs
- MS Access report data can be exported to MS Excel spreadsheet
- Staffing contact list updates contain only most recent data from the database

THE PRODUCT BACKLOG

User Stories are captured in a Product Backlog. There are several characteristics of the product backlog, which are important to understand:

1) The product backlog is a living document – items are added, changed, and/or removed from the backlog throughout the entire duration of the project.
2) All backlog items should be estimated – this is done in the form of user points which measure the effort required to complete the backlog item (as opposed to hours or man-hours)

3) All backlog items should be prioritized – prioritization may be based on risks, benefits/value, costs, or estimates (story points) and ensures the most important items are completed first
4) All backlog items should add value to the project – if items are determined not to add value, they should be omitted from the backlog
5) Backlog items may have varying level of detail – as iterative sprint planning occurs and items are selected for the upcoming sprint, these items will often have a more granular level of detail than other items

Product Backlog for New Payroll System			
Task ID	Story	Estimate	Priority
4	As a user, I want to enter my work hours so I can make sure I get paid on time	5	1
2	As an administrator, I want to approve timesheets so employees get paid	4	2
3	As a user, I want to log in to the system so I can perform payroll functions	4	3
1	As a user, I want to log off of the system so no one can enter erroneous information in my account	4	4
6	As an administrator, I want to run consolidated payroll reports so I can provide a weekly status to senior management	10	5
5	As an administrator, I want the ability to create new accounts so we can add employees after they're hired	7	6
8	As a user, I want the ability to edit my timesheet so I can correct any mistakes	5	7
7	As an administrator, I want the ability to set automated reminders so employees will verify and sign their timesheets on time	9	8
9	As an administrator, I want the ability to archive timesheets so the organization can file them for audit and tax purposes	15	9

References: Mike Cohn, *User Stories Applied*

LMS Functionality User Stories

1 Document Management and Editing

As a Faculty Member, I want...

to access the same online document as other users, so that learners can edit documents collaboratively.

multiple authors to edit the same document throughout the LMS environment, yet each does not have to log in to the LMS multiple times or in to multiple systems.

assignments submitted via the LMS to be searched for direct quotes, so that I can identify students and work with plagiarism.

to download completed assignments directly to my computer, so that I can edit files outside the LMS.

content fidelity (characters, formatting) after uploading my documents to the LMS, so I can use a the Macintosh versions of word processing tools.

to edit and save documents in the LMS, so that I do not have to download the file to my local desktop.

the screen to return to the area I was working after I submit/save, so that I do not have to scroll back down to where I was working from the top of the page when it refreshes.

to include programming code in my assignments, so they do not interfere with the functionality of the LMS yet the syntax/format/characters remain accurate.

As a Student, I want...

printer friendly formats for the LMS interfaces/tools, so I can work off line without losing content, context or wasting paper.

to save content from the LMS as a PDF, so I can protect my content from editing.

to export the content of a discussion, so that I can view, edit and save in a word processing application on my desktop.

to access other online services offered by my campus (e.g. tutoring, bookstore, library), so I can get feedback about my work directly from within the LMS.

no limit on the length of text I can write within a message reply, so I can write my entire paper in the LMS.

2 Communications

As a Faculty Member, I want...

access to communications (e.g. IM, Chat, Forums, etc.) tools outside of their, or any, section, so that students can communicate across multiple sections.

to identify specific discussion forum posts, so that I can grade the student responses.

to be notified whenever a new message is posted to a discussion I am subscribed to, so that I don't have to enter the LMS to check for each topic's updates.

to view a new discussion board message independently and individually without affecting the status (e.g. read, new, unread) of other posted messages, so that I don't have to read all of the new messages in one session.

to use [move] discussion topics and threads from another section to any other, so that I do not have to manually copy and paste from one course to the next.

to search course email by date, author, group, keyword, course/section and other criteria, so that I can find emails based on a specific and single attribute.

integrate external (e.g. personal or campus) and course emails from the LMS, so that students can respond to e-mail sent to them from the course without having to log onto the course web site to respond.

to post announcements, so that they get the immediate attention of my students while in the LMS.

send my language students voice messages, announcements to my students, so they can hear proper pronunciation and inflection.

to send a voice (audio) email within the course, so it is accessible in the site by faculty and students.

to push notifications to students through the LMS using external communications channels (e.g. email, IM, SMS, etc.), so that I do not need to log into the LMS to update my class.

to push notifications to students through the LMS using external communications channels (e.g. email, IM, SMS, etc.), so that my students don't have to log into the LMS to receive important updates.

to automatically send a notification to students when their grades/activity fall below a standard I set, so that students can adjust their behavior in order to complete/pass the course.

to have a course discussion that occurs outside of each section, so that students can learn from one another's field experiences across multiple sections.

As a Student, I want to...

view in one place all classmates that have contributed to a project, document activity, so that I can see what has been done and by whom.

view all assignments and due dates for a course in one place, so that I can identify what I need to do and when across the course.

to be notified via communications channels outside of the LMS, so that I can be reminded about approaching, class start dates, assignment due dates and exam dates.

set notification attributes, so I can define the time, frequency and type of alerts that are sent to me.

to be notified whenever a new message is posted to a discussion I am subscribed to, so that I don't have to enter the LMS to check for each topic's updates.

see who else is online in my course, so I can communicate with classmates and faculty in real time.

see who else is online across the LMS, so I can communicate with classmates and faculty in real time.

audio and video based synchronous communications, so that I can keep up with the class discussions without typing.

sort discussion posts, so that I can view the thread of a discussion.

to view course updates in my RSS reader, so I do not have to be in the LMS to find out about updates.

to post profile information about me, so other students and faculty can know more about each other.

to see all discussions in one view, so I can open any active discussion from the same page.

the professor to be notified via channels outside of the LMS, so they know when a student sends and email to them.

access to communications (e.g. IM, Chat, Forums, etc.) tools outside of my, or any, section, so that I can communicate across multiple sections with other students.

As a Librarian, I want...

access to independent synchronous communication tools within the LMS, so that I can work with students independent of a their courses.

3 Assessment & Grading

As a Faculty Member, I want...

to import exams/assessments and exam questions from external sources (e.g. as MS-Word documents), so that I don't have to reenter them in the LMS.

to import grades from other sources/systems, so that I can calculate a final graded including work that may have been done and assessed in another tool.

to calculate grades based on weighted averages, so that students always know their standing in the course.

to allow individual students to view individual grades, so that students can see their grades per assignment.

to allow individual students to view their course grades throughout the term, so they can see their standing in the course.

to scale and resize the grade book, so that I can see all of the students grades for the semester in one view.

various grading methods, so that I can grade based on points or letter grades.

to create formulas, so that I can convert points to letter grades.

to export grades in standard and popular file/exchange formats, so I can use external applications to manage my grades.

to create multiple versions of the same exam, so that questions can be randomized.

to create multiple versions of the same exam, so that multiple choice questions can be randomized.

to include private or public comments when grading a student's discussion post, so I do not have to email him/her separately.

to include private comments with all graded items, so I do not have to email students separately.

set up standardized grading criteria and standards, so I can score assignments subjectively related to learning objectives.

to associate/migrate grading criteria (rubrics, weights, formulas) with multiple sections, so I do not need to recreate them for each course/section.

to read a student's discussion posting, see the grading rubric and/or an email window at the same time, so I can write comments and calculate a grade while reading the postings.

to view the series of steps students undertake when solving calculation-based engineering/math problems, so I can assess problem solving.

a high-level math/scientific scripting language within all editors, so I can create text-based (not image-based) equations within the LMS.

to provide feed back and grades in voice threads, so that students can see comments and grades in the context of their work.

to set the time to finish a single test independently for individual students or groups, so that I can compensate for students with special needs without creating multiple tests.

to define when an exam is open (available) and closed in one form, so I do not need to navigate to other pages/forms.

the grade book to ignore assignments not yet due, so that the course grades reflect the students' current standing.

to allow students to grade their own or others work, so that I can see the reflection, assessment criteria and peers standards used by students.

to manually enter/overwrite grades in the grade book, so that the automatic calculations within the grade book or from the assignment are ignored.

to define grading criteria for each assignment and the course, so that the grade book automatically calculates final grades.

to return to my last edited entry in the gradebook so that I can quickly make my edits to my gradebook.

to use an evaluation tool that allows for mixing multiple choice and open-ended questions so that I can evaluate my students.

create learning experiences for my students that model a variety of different pedagogies, for example constructivism, active learning, student centered learning, collaborative learning, etc. so that we meet the needs of different learner styles and types.

As an Instructional Designer, I want...

would like to pass grades from the LMS to the SIS, so that faculty do not need to manually add their course grades.

As a Student, I want...

the option of showing everyone's grades in the class anonymously, so that students can compare their grades with the rest of the class.

to view my individual grades for assignments, so I can understand how my total grade is affected.

to view my course grades throughout the term, so I can see my standing in the course.

view all of my grades across all courses, so I so not need to enter each course.

As a Trainer, I want...

to use secure exam tools so that I can administer exam to both online and in-person students.

access subject-matter specific materials, so that I can become a more proficient trainer.

4 Course Management

As a Faculty Member, I want...

to add individual students who have not enrolled in my course section, so that they can audit the course.

to add access for tutors, so that they can assist students working in the course.

to manipulate items/icons on a course page using a simple drag-drop interface, so that I don't have to click through the LMS interface.

native drag and drop content directly from my desktop into my course sisette, so that I don't have to click the desktop operating system's navigational interface.

create learning experiences for my students that model a variety of different pedagogies, for example constructivism, active learning, student centered learning, collaborative learning, etc.,so that I can meet the needs of different learner styles and types.

varying content presented to different students in my course, so that I can construct individualized curricula for my students depending on assessment measures.

a "confirmation of receipt," so that I know that a student has received and opened an e-mail sent from the LMS.

to organize all of my course materials by weekly session, so that students can determine which assignments have been completed for each week in the proper order.

to toggle my course back and forth from faculty to student view, so I can verify that materials I've developed will function as designed.

to select multiple attributes associated with my course (including user ID, group membership, date range, and grade book results), so that I can control the visibility of course items.

to define release criteria for my content in my course, so that I can assign work to my students based on specific dates, to specific groups and/or specific grading criteria.

to create groups using sign-up sheets, so that students can self-identify for activities within the LMS.

to create groups of students within the course, so that I can manage their activities (access to content, tools).

to remove students from my course individually, so that I can remove students when they have dropped during the initial weeks of the semester.

to uploading files in two clicks, so that I do not need to navigate through various windows.

find a discussion post in two clicks, so that I do not need to navigate through various windows.

reset course materials for the next semester in two clicks, so that I do not need to navigate through various windows.

to publish multiple sections of the same course, so that uniform/standard content can be viewed by different users in different sections.

to administer course sections independently, so that modifications in one section do not affect other sections.

to track student participation in learning activities, so I can assess student engagement and time on task.

to view all input from an individual student from a single screen (e.g. see assignments, discussion posts, assessment attempts etc.), so that I can assess activity and completeness.

to create new courses/sections at any time and independent of the SIS, so I can develop course sites on the fly for my own use.

to save/transfer announcements from semester to semester, so that I can create a repository of effective messages for a class.

authorized users (e.g. faculty, course/department chair) to add access to courses, so that the department can facilitate peer observations.

set access time (start and end dates) for non-enrolled users (guests to the course), so that they can be removed without manual intervention.

students to work within the tools where assignments are delivered, so work their work is saved automatically and associated with the assignment (they do not have to attach their documents/drafts/final).

to download my course, so I can view my course off-line on my desktop computer.

to set access dates (opening and closing) for all discussions, so I do not need to individually open or close a discussion manually when the date arrives.

view compatible 3rd party/external applications/widgets within one location of the LMS, so I can add non-LMS native functionality to my course.

access to my courses from previous semesters, so I can use the old course format/content to start planning and building for the next semester.

to select old/current course content to populate new courses, so I do not have to manually add or create them again.

record the attendance in my in-person course in the LMS, so I can include participation in the online grade book.

to export reports on student activity, so I can share information with non LMS users.

to run reports on page use for various components of my course so that I can measure who's accessing what and for how long.

to globally change dates within my course for new semesters, so that I do not have to change each manually for each event/due-date.

access and change dates within my course through a single calendar view, so that I do not need to navigate to each event to change dates.

view all attributes associated with creating/releasing assignments, discussions, exams, etc., so I do not need to navigate to other pages to develop and distribute content.

to open access to all or some of my course (LMS tools, activities, content), so that the public can participate in my course.

access to permissions/attributes for each tool in the LMS, so that I can control which tools students have access to.

to toggle between courses so that I can control the visibility to all of my courses.

to migrate existing course material to new teaching and learning environment so that I can continue teaching online.

create learning experiences for my students that model a variety of different pedagogies, for example constructivism, active learning, student centered learning, collaborative learning, etc. so that we meet the needs of different learner styles and types.

have a learning platform that is accepted by QualityMatters.org so that distance learning courses can continue to gain approval from this organization.

As an LMS Administrator, I want...

to open access to all or some of the LMS courses (LMS tools, activities, content), so that the public can participate in the courses.

As a Student, I want...

open different sections in different windows of the LMS, so that I am able to view class materials from multiple courses/classes.

a "How do I..." glossary, so that I can look for answers to my problems.

to open multiple browser windows, so that I can see independent courses or parts of the same course in different windows.

to be notified of activity in the LMS via communications channels outside of the LMS, so that I know when changes to the course have been made.

to access the LMS from the SIS and/or my campus email account, so I do not have to log in again.

see the status of my assignments, so I can see work that is in progress or completed.

access to last year's course material so that I can prepare for my qualifying examination.

to have a calendar-based course site so that I can view all of my course material depending on the date.

to search across all of my courses so that I can easily access my course materials and information.

to have the same look and feel within a program or college so that my course will be consistent.

to search all courses simultaneously so that I can document that key concepts and objectives are being covered (in an environment where all courses are team taught).

to post an online searchable handbook so that users can download and easily print forms.

have a learning platform that allows me to get critical, up-to-the-minute SIS information about my student status such as registration data, grade reports, billing info. etc so that I don't have to log in separately.

have a more sophisticated, faster, and technologically advanced system that uses podcasts, lectures, and streams entertaining presentations that use animation so that I can get a better learning environment along with a better experience.

5 Content Management & Multi-Media

As a Faculty Member, I want...

to include audio and video files to my course, so that students can access each independently without leaving the LMS to use another application.

both students and me to create and save oral presentations (audio) from within the LMS, so that we do not need to log into other applications or upload 3rd party files.

access to a synchronous communications tool (e.g. real time audio, video, whiteboard, presentation, application sharing, break out rooms, and archiving capabilities) within the LMS, so I do not need to re-authenticate when moving between systems.

to upload and distribute media from different sources within the course, so that the location of the content is transparent to the instructor and students.

a student specific content repositories per course, so that submitted files can be segregated from other student work and retained in the course.

to sort student files in a course by author, date, title, etc., so that students and faculty can find files based on various known information.

to view the versions of submitted or collaborative work, so I can assess which edits where made by various contributors and when.

to access multiple drafts of content created in the LMS, so that my students and I can review previous work.

upload multiple files and file types per assignment, so I can present independent, but related documents and students can submit independent but related files.

to post homework assignments and solutions, so that my students have access to them.

to delete an incomplete post or mishandled assignment, so that so that it is not included in grading.

content created within the LMS during a course by students to be exportable, so that students can transport artifacts to other personal or institutional systems.

to open, comment on and save student documents, all with in the LMS, so that students can view my edits without downloading and uploading files.

to see the duration time of audio files accessible in the course, so I can sort recordings from longest to shortest.

edit content (tests or assessments) within the LMS after students have submitted work, so I can correct errors and republish rather than create new tests/assignments.

to export my course materials, so that any other instructor in my institution can use them.

drag and drop assignment/content, so that I do not need to click a series of buttons/links/pages to order my documents/activities.

to group media content uploaded to the LMS, so that I can see objects in relationship to each section, course, user.

a standards based interface, so I can import course content from publishers, test generators, or other sources.

to allow peers access to selected work, so that students can review one another's work.

access and store content independently of the course/section, directly from within the LMS, so I do not need to log into or navigate to another system.

embed (not just link) Web 0 technologies, so I can customize my course with existing technologies.

to model face to face interactions online so that I can have small group work sessions and large group facilitated discussions.

As an Instructional Designer, I want...

to upload a file, multiple files or all files in a folder at once, so I do not have to upload files individually.

As a Librarian, I want...

to embed library e-reserves directly in courses, so students and faculty do not need to log into another system to access content.

a repository to upload cross-course resources, so faculty, nor I, need to load it into each course/section.

As a Student, I want...

to provide access to my content, tools and activities to other students, so I can collaborate with student teams within the course.

to access synchronous communication tools within a course and outside of a course, so that I can work with classmates on my own.

embed (not just link) Web 0 technologies, so I can customize my course with existing technologies.

to accomplish course administrative tasks (like uploading files, finding a discussion post, resetting course material for the next semester, etc.) in two clicks from within the specific feature, so that I can maintain a contextual work flow.

to create a portfolio, so that I can selectively extract content from any of my courses and allow external visitors to view it.

the LMS to save my work automatically and periodically, so that I can access my previous work without it being lost due to a timeout or outage.

a "light" version of the system, so that my dial-up connection will not get bogged down.

a mobile version of the system, so that I can access my courses on my hand held device

standards compliant audio/video formats available through multiple players, so that I can use my own audio/video player (desktop, hand held) to listen to class audio/video files.

video or lecture capture within the LMS, so that I do not need to access (perhaps logging into) multiple systems.

the files I post to reflect the time zone that I am in, so that I do not lose out on the amount of time to complete assignments.

the files posted my others (including faculty) to reflect the time zone that I am in, so that I do not lose out on the amount of time to view materials.

to move the tools within the interface, so that I can to avoid "scrolling" the window.

to view all of my course lectures, so that I can determine their order within the course.

a single reference for all of my courses, so I can see (and access) current due dates for assignments and tests/quizzes, and updates when due dates change.

new notifications for new content and grades to disappear after I have looked at them, so I know what is still awaiting review.

to aggregate dates associated with LMS content and activity with my other calendars, so I can view personal and academic events despite which calendar I am in.

archive my courses, so that I can access content from within.

create and maintain local archives and backups, so that I can store and access course content despite my campuses or systems policies.

to share my uploaded documents and LMS-specific content through the LMS, so my classmates can work with me in our own study groups.

personal areas to develop and store content, so others cannot access my class notes, drafts, uploaded files, etc.

to submit multiple drafts of assignments through the LMS, so instructors can provide feedback before the final grade for the assignment.

to access campus related links in (# of clicks) so that I can easily locate relevant articles.

to take an online course from another campus so that I don't have to apply to their program and get a second ID.

6 Accessibility & Usability

As a Faculty Member, I want...

user-adjustable font sizes and audio tools, so that students with special needs can access my course and content.

to tailor the interface and functionality, so that I can employ principles of universal design in the development of my course.

access the LMS in any browser, so that I can work on my course from any networked computer.

to customize the icons for tools in my course, so I and students can set up the user interface to our personal preferences.

to customize the icons for tools in my language courses, so that students can work in the language of study.

cross-platform compatibility, so that I can use the LMS on multiple devices and computers (PC/Mac/Linux, hand helds, smartphones, tablets).

508 and WAI compliant and certification, so that I can conform with local, state and federal accessibility policies and regulations.

FERPA complaint security, so that I can conform with local, state and federal policies and regulations.

As a Student, I want

to contact someone over the phone for troubleshooting, so that I can talk to a human being and get the problem fixed faster and easier.

access help, tips/tricks from within each tool/feature, so that I can get help in context to the LMS functionality.

to allow students to change their username within the course to a nickname, so that students don't have to show their full name.

to access, review and edit the course through audio only, so that visually impaired students can participate in online courses.

non-visual cues/interfaces for all activities undertaken in the LMS and the content delivered through it, so that I can access all functionality and materials within the course.

7 System Administration

As an LMS Administrator, I want...

to add individual students who have not enrolled in my course section, so that they can audit the course.

to restrict course design to a lead teacher, so that other instructors of a section teaching that course cannot alter specific elements.

to provide templates for courses, so that the look and feel within a program or college can be consistent.

to view all links to an individual resource from the source item, so I can click a file to see where in the course it is being used.

the option to delete the source file/activity when the link to the file/activity is deleted, so I do not have orphaned files in the system.

to move or rename files, so that links do not break.

to upload a file, multiple files or all files in a folder at once, so I do not have to upload files individually.

upload files via common standards from within the LMS, so that I do not have to use multiple applications.

a unique identifier associated with files, so I can identify the person who uploaded a file.

file creation/modified dates to remain intact after a course is copied for reuse in subsequent semesters, so I can find the history of files.

warnings for html files that have encodings that do not match_, so that errors can be addressed before course pages are published publicly._

to parse file names when uploading, so that improper formatting can be detected.

to export content or learning activities in the course in standard formats (e.g. SCORM, Common Cartridge, pdf, .docx, .rtf) with the option to include student content, so that learning objects and archived materials may be used in the future.

to export documents from the course in standard formats (e.g. SCORM, Common Cartridge, pdf, .docx, .rtf) with the option to include student content, so that learning objects and archived materials may be used independantly on the desktop in a office productivity tools.

to create/edit html documents through the LMS or a third-party html editor without leaving the LMS, so that I do not have to manage multiple applications, file copies or logins.

to set the page I return to after undertaking an activity (clicking "Submit" or "Save" in a form), so that I do not have to navigate from the system's default refresh page.

to bookmark specific pages, so I can return to pages where I undertake common tasks.

cross list the same course, so that one course or one section can be offered by different academic departments.

batch upload my students and my courses either on a " as requested basis" or all at once, so I do not need to manually and individually make modifications to the course/section/LMS.

to pass userid's and passwords from other campus enterprise applications to the LMS, so users do not need to remember multiple logins.

to retain student data when students are un-enrolled from courses, so that I can review their activity and content when they are no longer able to access the course/section/LMS.

to back and restore courses and content (individually and in bulk), so that I can provide faculty with up-to-date versions of their courses and content in case they lose or delete information.

to query courses, so that I can find specific students names, groups, file names/types, text strings, dates, etc.

an open database, so that I can construct my own data queries and reports or modify the systems default queries/reports.

define the features (tools, functionality) at the institutional level, so I do not need to go into each course to add or remove tools/features/functionality individually.

setup default grading schema at the institution level, so I do not need to set up grading in each course/section individually.

to implement custom branding at the institutional and departmental levels, so I do not need to edit each course/section individually.

to pass enrollment information automatically from the SIS, so that courses, students, etc. are updated in real-time and I do not need to manage batch uploads.

to integrate the LMS with identity management standards (e.g. CAS, Shibboleth, etc.), so that I can manage authentication and authorization consistently across all of my campus services.

to provide users with immediate course registration so that users can quickly access their content.

access, assess, and manage permissions for ePortfolio content directly from within the LMS, so I do not need to log into or navigate to another system.

to have a system that allows incomplete access for individual students once a course has closed.

to use discussion topics from another section so that I do not have to manually copy and paste from one course to the next.

to need to track authorship of course content as course sections are copied and edited over the life of a course.

As an Instructional Designer, I want...

to automate the creation of a blank course shells for every course, so that faculty are not required to fill out a form.

to automate the creation of a blank course shells for every course, so that administrators do not have to create batches for course shell creation by hand.

to enter_/view_ courses without enrolling in the course roster, so I do not appear in areas like the grade book, student roster, etc.

to manage enrollments and privileges to courses from a central location, so I do not have to log in to or access each course separately.

to integrate with external and internal resources with a single sign on (e.g. content management, wikis, blogs, eportfolio, directory services, student information systems, etc.), so that users do not have to log in multiple times to multiple systems.

to pass information from and to the SIS through common and diverse methods simultaneously within the same instance, so that campuses can use integration methods within their capacity and resources.

a system with contextually-sensitive help combined with built-in screencast tutorials for better self-help remediation.

8 Migration

As an Instructional Designer, I want...

to import courses archived from other LMS's, so that we can respond quickly and efficiently to faculty requests for new course shells from legacy systems or systems on other campuses.

to batch import archived courses from other LMS's, so that we can respond quickly and efficiently to faculty requests for new course shells from legacy systems or systems on other campuses.

to script translation criteria and batch load courses for migration, so that I do not need to manually address each course to be converted.

an standardized implementation plan that has been tested and verifiable from other similar institutions, so that the campuses can be up and running with an LMS solution within 18 months

3 Administrative and Technical Requirements

3.1 Application Administration

As an LMS administrator, I want...

access to individual user accounts (profiles/attributes) within the LMS, so that I can make manually view and update users, information, roles, sections, courses, enrollments.

to create individual user accounts (profiles/attributes) within the LMS, so that I add users, information, roles, sections and courses outside of the batch process.

system-wide access to UID, groups, courses, sections, so that I can manually resolve issues.

access to LMS vendor-sponsored/supported technical training, so that I can stay abreast of the technical developments required to support the LMS.

to participate in peer-to-peer communities of practice, so that I can learn from and communicate with other LMS users.

to send announcements to users of the system so they can be informed of system outages, issues or scheduled maintenance events.

3.2 Identity Management: Authentication & Authorization

As an LMS administrator, I want...

the LMS to authenticate against external LDAP sources, so that hosted campuses can manage their own users and credentials.

to set user authentication independently of, and in addition to, external LDAP sources, so that I can set local access.

to pass authentication and authorization from the LMS, so that courses can include third-party tools.

3.3 Course, Section, User Batching

As an LMS administrator, I want...

a secure FTP directory that multiple unique campuses can upload batch files to, so that the LMS can access and create courses.

a secure FTP directory that multiple unique campuses can upload batch files to, so that the LMS can access and create users.

a secure FTP directory that multiple unique campuses can upload batch files to, so that the LMS can access and create roles (instructional designers, instructors, students, LMS administrators, teaching assistants, auditors, help desk staff).

batched users to be enrolled in their courses by the LMS, so we and the campuses do not have to do it manually.

3.4 Backup

As an LMS administrator, I want...

to back up individual active sections on a weekly bases, so that UMassOnline can restore individual courses and course content on demand.

to archive individual sections on a semester bases from the LMS, so that UMassOnline can distribute courses/sections/content to the campuses for archiving.

a back-up of the entire database, so that UMassOnline can restore our implementation for disaster recovery.

3.5 Continuity

As a technical operations manager, I want...

to be notified when LMS service interruptions occur, so that I can notify our stakeholders.

to be notified when LMS service is depreciated, so that I can notify our stakeholders.

users to fail over upon a service outage to a redundant environment, so that I can ensure continued availability of the LMS.

to sync my production and disaster recovery environments, so that I can ensure data continuity at the time of a disaster.

to stand up a new primary production environment in the event of a disaster within one day, so that we will have minimal down time.

a pre-defined maintenance and upgrade schedule, so I can coordinate with multiple campuses maintenance windows and upgrades in a consistent manner.

real time notifications, so I can communicate with users immediately of system issues while they are logged in to the LMS.

to emulate the user experience (all roles), so that I can monitor the health of the LMS periodically.

to monitor LMS resource consumption (CPU, bandwidth I/O, data base I/O, etc.), so that I can ascertain health of the system and its resources.

to review LMS resource consumption (CPU, bandwidth I/O, data base I/O, etc.), so I can diagnose service degradation and interruptions.

to monitor user activity (active users, http requests, sessions open, etc.), so I can assess systems performance based on demand.

to access feature by feature comparisons related to functional upgrades so that I can train and support end-users in a context that is familiar to them.

3.6 Systems Integration

As an LMS administrator, I want...

to expose available third-party tools through the internal LMS tool set, so that faculty can find available tools within the LMS itself.

to pass course/section attributes (user identity, section enrollment, course information, etc.) from the LMS, so that courses can include third-party tools.

to include contact information (email, chat and phone) within each page of a course section, so that users can connect directly through the LMS to support services.

to integrate with campus student information systems frequently, so UMassOnline that can ensure the timely transfer of data.

to create courses, sections and users (all roles) in real time, so campuses can provide on-demand enrollments.

to provide access to third-party tools (Helix, Wimba, SafeAssign, Scholar, Respondus, Voice Tools) from within the LMS, so that users can move seamlessly between UMassOnline's current portfolio of systems.

to transfer files between the LMS and third-party tools (Helix, Wimba, SafeAssign, Scholar, Respondus, Voice Tools), so that content can move seamlessly between UMassOnline's current portfolio of systems.

to integrate the internal email of the LMS and the email address of record in the student information system (or another preferred email address), so users can manage a single email account.

access within the LMS to all data fields published by the student information system, so I can create standard or customized levels and points of integration.

3.7 User Activity and Performance Reporting

As an LMS administrator, I want...

to query the number of logged in users via the LMS, so that we can assess current and historical load measurements.

to query the frequency LMS specific tools are used, via the LMS, so that we can understand user activity and potentially needs (training, technical, 3rd party tools, etc.) for enhancements.

to assess LMS activity (time on task/page), student activity (enter/exit page), enrollments, sections, and tool/item use via the LMS, so that we can generate general utilization reports and specifically determine if access has been attained by users.

to search sections and users based on the LMS's attributes/criteria, via the LMS, so that we can build ad hoc reports.

to design and modify existing default reports, via the LMS, so that we can build ad hoc reports.

to query LMS generated schema/data via an open database, so that I can run reports via a third party reporting tool.

3.8 Testing & QA

As an LMS QA technician, I want...

to access a test environment that emulates our production environment, so I can assess reported issues/bugs, updates, patches, enhancements, etc. without affecting the production environment and our active users.

to view the LMS as multiple user-types in the same login session without logging in and out, so that I can emulate our user's experiences and test functionality across the system.

to participate in beta and cohort programs so I can evaluate patches and fixes alongside a community of peers.

3.9 Training

As a system-wide trainer, I want...

to provide campuses with training materials that focus on side-by-side feature comparisons with Blackboard Vista, so that UMassOnline and our supported campuses can train campuses in the new LMS environment.

to modify vendor created training materials, so I can address UMassOnline's unique service environment that campuses have up-to-date, authoritative reference materials per patch, dotX version, service packs, etc.

to modify vendor created training materials, so I can address UMassOnline's unique service/support environment.

access to LMS vendor-sponsored/supported training related to pedagogical (teaching and learning) affordances, so that I can educate local campus trainers and faculty on how to support unique teaching styles.

access to LMS vendor-sponsored/supported functional training, so that UMassOnline can educate local campus trainers and end-users with point and click functionality.

to participate in peer-to-peer communities of practice, so that I can learn from, and communicate with, other campuses using the same LMS.

access to LMS vendor-sponsored/supported technical training, so I can stay up to date on administrative, integration and technical issues.

in-line contextual help, so that users can resolve their own usability/feature/functionality issues.

prompts/hints when users mouse-over objects, so that users can learn about previously, or infrequently, used tools/features.

to provide users access to tips and tricks, so that users can become more proficient with the LMS.

access for all users to a community of practice, so they can learn from peers.

user to have access to subject-matter specific tutorials, so that users can become more proficient.

3.10 Technical and End User Support

As an LMS administrator, I want...

to contribute our local technical and user support discoveries to the support provider, so that their knowledge base reflects current issues/understanding/resolutions of the user community.

to download release notes from a secure web site to create testable scripts, so I can assess production readiness for hotfixes, patches, service packs and upgrades.

As a support analyst, I want...

access to a ticketing system, so that I can report to, update, search for, etc. issues directly with the service provider.

issue status (eg: bug tracking/resolution) communications through the ticketing system, so that I can document and communicate to my end-users.

to include multiple user types from our community in service requests/tickets, so that affected users are communicated regarding status updates and during issue resolution.

to participate in peer-to-peer communities of practice, so that I can learn from and communicate with other LMS users.

to access the system under different roles in the same login session, so I do not have to log out and back in several times to assess issues.

to reach a support technician immediately, so I can report system outages 24/

to reach a support technician within 30 minutes, so I can report performance degradation that falls below the SLA.

to reach a support technician within 30 minutes, so I can report when major components (content/activity) are unavailable/unusable.

to reach a support technician within 1 hour, so I can report when minor components (formatting/functionality) are operating abnormally.

to reach a support technician within 30 minutes, so I can report performance degradation that falls below the SLA.

to propose product enhancements/feature requests, so I can help direct and shape product development to meet our users' needs.

4 Program Management

4.1 Communications

As a Academic Program Manager, I want...

to send messages/announcements through the LMS based on course/student attributes (course, program, status, major, etc), so we can target specific student populations.

to determine who is online and accessing course content/activities, so I can verify submitted work.

4.2 Budgeting

As an Academic Program Manager, I want...

access to contracted pricing and services, so that pricing is stable and service is constant over time.

4.3 Quality

As an Academic Program Manager, I want...

to provide access to departmental staff, so I can conduct peer reviews of courses.

4.4 Service & Support

As an Academic Program Manager, I want...

performance and response definitions with criteria and metrics, so that service and support can be monitored, measured and reported to any interested stakeholders.

performance and response definitions with remedies for degraded service, so that the campus has recourse for poor service/support.

to verify ADA compliance, so I can meet University, State and Federal regulations.

4.5 Training

As an Instructional Designer, I want...

to cover fundamental training on the new LMS features and functionality_ for faculty in two hours, so that they can deliver a recently migrated course as is.

training resources, including syllabi/ outlines, powerpoints, tutorials, and QuickStart guides, so I do not have to develop them on my own.

Cape Project Management, Inc.

Agile Glossary

Note: The following Agile terms and definitions are primarily excerpts from web pages or books. I do not retain the copyright for any of this work. All copyrights reside with their respective authors, web pages or publishers. All other brands or product names used in this Guide are the trade names or registered trademarks of their respective owners.

Agile Contracting	The first lesson we learnt in contracting out agile software development (or anything else for that matter), is to align objectives of the supplier and the customer. It is highly desirable to align supplier success with customer success. The key here is to define the product vision and what must be achieved; foster shared ownership of the goals by treating your supplier as a partner; and consider offering the supplier incentives for meeting key business performance indicators that require partnership with you. http://blog.scrumup.com/2012/11/top-ten-reads-on-agile-contracts.html
Agile Discovery	During the Discovery Phase, designers need to work with the business analyst to capture and define business requirements. This is done by facilitating workshops and interviewing key stakeholders. A lot of sketching, note taking, brainstorming and discussion happen at this stage in order to effectively visualize the early thinking on look and feel, layout and interaction design. It is also worth noting that defining the business model is an evolutionary process. At the end of the discovery and design phases the value proposition needs to map back to real user personas, partnerships, activities, a cost structure, solid business KPIs and have a business mission statement should all clearly defined. https://www.arrkgroup.com/thought-leadership/the-importance-of-getting-the-discovery-phase-right/
Architectural Spike	XP does this while the initial Planning Game is in process. It's not an iteration - it might be longer or shorter, we don't know yet. What it's about is exploring solution elements that seem relevant to the as yet limited knowledge we have about the problem domain, choosing a System Metaphor, putting enough of our build, dbms, and source control tools in place to be able to begin controlled work, and then proceeding until we have something that runs and can be iterated. https://www.linkedin.com/pulse/agile-architecting-practice-architecture-spike-erik-philippus
Active Listening	Active listening is a communication technique used in counselling, training and conflict resolution, which requires the listener to feed back what they hear to the speaker, by way of re-stating or paraphrasing what they have heard in their own words, to confirm what they have heard and moreover, to confirm the understanding of both parties https://en.wikipedia.org/wiki/Active_listening
Adaptive Leadership	Adaptive leadership focuses on team management, from building self-organizing teams to developing a servant leadership style. It is both more difficult, and ultimately more rewarding than managing tasks. In an agile enterprise the people take care of the tasks and the leader engages the people. The facilitative leader works on things like building self-organizing teams, a trusting and respectful environment, collaboration, participatory decision making, and developing appropriate empowerment guidelines (for an excellent discussion of empowerment, see Chapters 6 & 7 in (Appelo, 2011)). https://www.infoq.com/news/2011/02/highsmith-adaptive-leadership Appelo, J. (2011). Management 3.0: Leading Agile Developers, Developing Agile Leaders. Upper Saddle River, JN: Addison-Wesley.

Adaptability, Three Components	Adaptability has three components—**product, process, and people.** You need to have a gung-ho agile team with the right attitude about change. You need processes and practices that allow the team to adapt to circumstances. And you *need* high quality code with automated tests. You can have pristine code and a non-agile team and change will be difficult. All three are required to have an agile, adaptable environment. http://searchsoftwarequality.techtarget.com/feature/Adaptation-in-project-management-through-agile
Affinity Estimating	A facilitated process where team members for sequence the product backlog from smallest to largest user story, then the rest of the team validates and finally the user stories are group by a sizing method such as t-shirt size or Fibonacci sequence. http://www.gettingagile.com/2008/07/04/affinity-estimating-a-how-to/
Agile Product Lifecycle	**The Five Agile plans:** 1 – Product Vision: Yearly By Product Owner 2 – Product Roadmap: Bi-Yearly By The Product Owner 3 – Release Plan: Quarterly By The Product Owner And Teams 4 – Iteration Plan: Bi-Weekly By The Teams 5 – Daily Plan (Scrum): Daily By Individual (EXAM TIP: different authors reference different time periods for updating these plans) https://www.ramantech.com/implementing-the-5-levels-of-agile-planning/ http://www.romanpichler.com/blog/
Agile Modeling (AM)	AM is a collection of values, principles, and practices for modeling software that can be applied on a software development project in an effective and light-weight manner. Values: 1. Communication 2. Simplicity 3. Feedback 4. Courage 5. Humility Principles/Practices: • Active Stakeholder Participation. Stakeholders should provide information in a timely manner, make decisions in a timely manner, and be as actively involved in the development process through the use of inclusive tools and techniques. • Architecture Envisioning. At the beginning of an agile project you will need to do some initial, high-level architectural modeling to identify a viable technical strategy for your solution. • Document Continuously. Write deliverable documentation throughout the lifecycle in parallel to the creation of the rest of the solution. • Document Late. Write deliverable documentation as late as possible, avoiding speculative ideas that are likely to change in favor of stable information. • Executable Specifications. Specify requirements in the form of executable "customer tests", and your design as executable developer tests, instead of non-executable "static" documentation. • Iteration Modeling. At the beginning of each iteration you will do a bit of modeling as

	part of your iteration planning activities. • Just Barely Good Enough (JBGE) artifacts. A model or document needs to be sufficient for the situation at hand and no more. • Look Ahead Modeling. Sometimes requirements that are nearing the top of your priority stack are fairly complex, motivating you to invest some effort to explore them before they're popped off the top of the work item stack so as to reduce overall risk. • Model Storming. Throughout an iteration you will model storm on a just-in-time (JIT) basis for a few minutes to explore the details behind a requirement or to think through a design issue. • Multiple Models. Each type of model has its strengths and weaknesses. An effective developer will need a range of models in their intellectual toolkit enabling them to apply the right model in the most appropriate manner for the situation at hand. • Prioritized Requirements. Agile teams implement requirements in priority order, as defined by their stakeholders, so as to provide the greatest return on investment (ROI) possible. • Requirements Envisioning. At the beginning of an agile project you will need to invest some time to identify the scope of the project and to create the initial prioritized stack of requirements. • Single Source Information. Strive to capture information in one place and one place only. • Test-Driven Design (TDD). Write a single test, either at the requirements or design level, and then just enough code to fulfill that test. TDD is a JIT approach to detailed requirements specification and a confirmatory approach to testing. http://www.agilemodeling.com/
Agile Scaling Model	Agile scaling factors are: 1. Team size 2. Geographical distribution 3. Regulatory compliance 4. Domain complexity 5. Organizational distribution 6. Technical complexity 7. Organizational complexity 8. Enterprise discipline https://www.agilealliance.org/wp-content/uploads/2016/01/Agile-Scaling-Model.pdf
Agile Triangle	The three dimensions critical to Agile performance measurement : • Value, • Quality • Constraints (cost, schedule, scope). Also, simplified to be: • Value • Technical debt • Cost http://jimhighsmith.com/beyond-scope-schedule-and-cost-the-agile-triangle/
APM Delivery Framework	However, if the business objective is reliable innovation, then the process framework must be organic, flexible, and easy to adapt. The APM process framework supports this second business objective through the five phases of:

	<ul><li>Envision</li><li>Speculate</li><li>Explore</li><li>Adapt</li><li>Close</li></ul> http://www.informit.com/articles/article.aspx?p=174660&seqNum=4
Asynchronous Builds	When you use the integration script discussed earlier, you're using synchronous integration—you're confirming that the build and tests succeed before moving on to your next task. If the build is too slow, synchronous integration becomes untenable. (For me, 20 or 30 minutes is too slow.) In this case, you can use asynchronous integration instead. Rather than waiting for the build to complete, start your next task immediately after starting the build, without waiting for the build and tests to succeed. The biggest problem with asynchronous integration is that it tends to result in broken builds. If you check in code that doesn't work, you have to interrupt what you're doing when the build breaks half an hour or an hour later. If anyone else checked out that code in the meantime, their build won't work either. If the pair that broke the build has gone home or to lunch, someone else has to clean up the mess. In practice, the desire to keep working on the task at hand often overrides the need to fix the build. If you have a very slow build, asynchronous integration may be your only option. If you must use this, a continuous integration server is the best way to do so. It will keep track of what to build and automatically notify you when the build has finished. http://jamesshore.com/Agile-Book/continuous_integration.html
Backlog Grooming/ Refinement	Product Backlog refinement is the act of adding detail, estimates, and order to items in the Product Backlog. This is an ongoing process in which the Product Owner and the Development Team collaborate on the details of Product Backlog items. During Product Backlog refinement, items are reviewed and revised. The Scrum Team decides how and when refinement is done. Refinement usually consumes no more than 10% of the capacity of the Development Team. However, Product Backlog items can be updated at any time by the Product Owner or at the Product Owner's discretion. http://www.scrumguides.org/scrum-guide.html
Brainstorming	A brainstorming session is a tool to generate ideas from a selected audience to solve a problem or stimulate creativity. These meetings are used for solving a process problem, inventing new products or product innovation, solving inter-group communication problems, improving customer service, budgeting exercises, project scheduling, etc. Using these tools can help discussion facilitators and Project Managers with alternative approaches for creative idea generation meetings (aka Brainstorming Sessions). They are particularly useful when previous meetings have gone afoul, are not as effective as they could be or productivity during these exercises is less than it should be. http://www.projectconnections.com/templates/detail/brainstorming-meeting-techniques.html
Burn Down Charts	<table><tr><td>X-Axis</td><td>The project/iteration timeline</td></tr></table>

	Y-Axis	The work that needs to be completed for the project. The time estimates for the work remaining will be represented by this axis.
	Project Start Point	This is the farthest point to the left of the chart and occurs at day 0 of the project/iteration.
	Project End Point	This is the point that is farthest to the right of the chart and occurs on the predicted last day of the project/iteration
	Ideal Work Remaining Line	This is a straight line that connects the start point to the end point. At the start point, the ideal line shows the sum of the estimates for all the tasks (work) that needs to be completed. At the end point, the ideal line intercepts the x-axis showing that there is no work left to be completed.
	Actual Work Remaining Line	This shows the actual work remaining. At the start point, the actual work remaining is the same as the ideal work remaining but as time progresses; the actual work line fluctuates above and below the ideal line depending on how effective the team is. In general, a new point is added to this line each day of the project. Each day, the sum of the time estimates for work that was recently completed is subtracted from the last point in the line to determine the next point.
	Actual Work Line is above the Ideal Work Line	If the actual work line is above the ideal work line, it means that there is more work left than originally predicted and the project is behind schedule.
	Actual Work Line is below the Ideal Work Line	If the actual work line is below the ideal work line, it means that there is less work left than originally predicted and the project is ahead of schedule.

http://en.wikipedia.org/wiki/Burn_down_chart

Burndown Bar Charts	The typical Scrum release burndown bar chart shows a single value--the net change in the amount of work remaining.
	<ul><li>As tasks are completed, the top of the bar is lowered.</li><li>When tasks are added to the original set, the bottom of the bar is lowered.</li><li>When tasks are removed from the original set, the bottom of the bar is raised.</li><li>When the amount of work involved in a task changes, the top of the bar moves up or down.</li></ul>

	https://www.mountaingoatsoftware.com/agile/scrum/scrum-tools/release-burndown/alternative
Burn Up Charts	The amount of accepted work (that work which has been completed, tested, and met acceptance criteria) is graphed in a burnup chart. The amount of work in an accepted state starts at 0 and continues to grow until it reaches 100% accepted at the end of the Iteration. http://www.clariostechnology.com/productivity/blog/whatisaburnupchart
Chartering in Agile	1. **Vision:** The vision defines the "Why" of the project. This is the higher purpose, or the reason for the project's existence. 2. **Mission:** This is the "What" of the project and it states what will be done in the project to achieve its higher purpose. 3. **Success Criteria:** The success criteria are management tests that describe effects outside of the solution itself. https://www.infoq.com/news/2010/05/agile-project-charter
Collaboration	Collaboration is the basis for bringing together the knowledge, experience and skills of multiple team members to contribute to the development of a new product more effectively than individual team members performing their narrow tasks in support of product development. As such collaboration is the basis for concepts such as concurrent engineering or integrated product development.

	Effective collaboration requires actions on multiple fronts:
	• Early involvement and the availability of resources to effectively collaborate
	• A culture that encourages teamwork, cooperation and collaboration
	• Effective teamwork and team member cooperation
	• Defined team member responsibilities based on collaboration
	• A defined product development process based on early sharing of information and collaborating
	• Collocation or virtual collocation
	• Collaboration technology
	(EXAM TIP: There was specifically a question about the difference between coordination and collaboration)
	http://www.npd-solutions.com/collaboration.html
Collaboration Games	Agile games are activities focused on teaching, demonstrating, and improving Agile and organizational effectiveness using game theory. Using games, we can model complex or time-consuming processes and systems, examine why they work (or don't work), look for improvements, and teach others how to benefit from them. Games can model just the core of a process or model, leaving out unimportant factors. They can involve collaboration, brainstorming, comparing variants, and of course retrospectives.

http://tastycupcakes.org/ |
| **Collective Code Ownership** | The way this works is for each developer to create unit tests for their code as it is developed. All code that is released into the source code repository includes unit tests that run at 100%. Code that is added, bugs as they are fixed, and old functionality as it is changed will be covered by automated testing. Now you can rely on the test suite to watch dog your entire code repository. Before any code is released it must pass the entire test suite at 100%. Once this is in place anyone can make a change to any method of any class and release it to the code repository as needed. When combined with frequent integration developers rarely even notice a class has been extended or repaired.

http://www.extremeprogramming.org/rules/collective.html |
| **Collocated And Or Distributed Teams** | Collocated Agile is a model in which projects execute the Agile Methodology with teams located in a single room. The methodology requires that the complete team be in close proximity to each other to improve coordination between the members. Collocated Agile teams have proven that the real power of project success lies not in administration, but in the acumen, chemistry, loyalty, and dedication between the collocated teams.
Distributed Agile, as the name implies, is a model in which projects execute an Agile Methodology with teams that are distributed across multiple geographies.

http://www.continuousagile.com/unblock/team_options.html |
| **Compliance** | Agile allows faster time to market by deploying working code more quickly. Application of user stories and iterations in a regulated industry can help to keep the team focused for large projects. Compliance regulations or legislation can sometimes change quickly. The opportunity to more easily cater for change gives the business stakeholders value earlier. As requirements change there is an avoidance of waste, due to not designing and detailing all requirements upfront.
A successful agile compliance project requires the right people, the right team culture and the right amount of regulation / industry knowledge in the team. |

	A tool may assist in enabling the appropriate levels of communication and reporting – so that the status of the project can be easily visible. Various considerations for agile projects in a regulated industry have been discussed here. Although there may be challenges, for a team with the right focus and frame of mind it is a matter of "where there is a will there is a way". Some areas may need to be adapted – however that merely seems to be in line with the whole essence and concept of what agile is all about – agility and responsiveness. https://www.planittesting.com/us/Insights/2012/Agile-and-Regulatory-Compliance
Conflict Resolution	Principles to Remember Do: Set up conflict management procedures before a conflict arises Intervene early when a fight erupts between team members Get the team working together again as soon as possible Don't: Assume your team agrees on its shared purpose, values, or vision Let conflicts fester or go unattended Move on without first talking about the conflict as a team https://hbr.org/2010/06/get-your-team-to-stop-fighting.html
Conflict Levels	**Level 1: Problem to Solve** We all know what conflict at level 1 feels like. Everyday frustrations and aggravations make up this level, and we experience conflicts as they rise and fall and come and go. At this level, people have different opinions, misunderstanding may have happened, conflicting goals or values may exist, and team members likely feel anxious about the conflict in the air. When in level 1, the team remains focused on determining what's awry and how to fix it. Information flows freely, and collaboration is alive. Team members use words that are clear, specific, and factual. The language abides in the here and now, not in talking about the past. Team members check in with one another if they think a miscommunication has just happened. You will probably notice that team members seem optimistic, moving through the conflict. It's not comfortable, but it's not emotionally charged, either. Think of level 1 as the level of constructive disagreement that characterizes high-performing teams. **Level 2: Disagreement** At level 2, self-protection becomes as important as solving the problem. Team members distance themselves from one another to ensure they come out OK in the end or to establish a position for compromise they assume will come. They may talk offline with other team members to test strategies or seek advice and support. At this level, good-natured joking moves toward the half-joking barb. Nastiness gets a sugarcoating but still comes across as bitter. Yet, people aren't hostile, just wary. Their language reflects this as their words move from the specific to the general. Fortifying their walls, they don't share all they know about the issues. Facts play second fiddle to interpretations and create confusion about what's really happening. **Level 3: Contest** At level 3, the aim is to win. A compounding effect occurs as prior conflicts and problems remain unresolved. Often, multiple issues cluster into larger issues or create a "cause." Factions emerge in this fertile ground from which misunderstandings and power politics arise. In an agile team, this may happen subtly, because a hallmark of working agile is the feeling that we are all in this together. But it does happen. People begin to align themselves with one side or the other. Emotions become tools used to

"win" supporters for one's position. Problems and people become synonymous, opening people up to attack. As team members pay attention to building their cases, their language becomes dis-torted. They make overgeneralizations: "He always forgets to check in his code" or "You never listen to what I have to say." They talk about the other side in presumptions: "I know what they think, but they are ignoring the real issue." Views of themselves as benevolent and others as tarnished become magnified: "I am always the one to compromise for the good of the team" or "I have everyone's best interest at heart" or "They are intentionally ignoring what the customer is really saying." Discussion becomes either/or and blaming flourishes. In this combative environment, talk of peace may meet resistance. People may not be ready to move beyond blaming.

Level 4: Crusade

At level 4, resolving the situation isn't good enough. Team members believe the people on the "other side" of the issues will not change. They may believe the only option is to remove the others from the team or get removed from the team themselves. Factions become entrenched and can even solidify into a pseudo-organizational structure within the team. Identifying with a faction can overshadow identifying with the team as a whole so the team's identity gets trounced. People and positions are seen as one, opening up people to attack for their affiliations rather than their ideas. These attacks come in the form of language rife with ideology and principles, which becomes the focus of conversation, rather than specific issues and facts. The overall attitude is righteous and punitive.

Level 5: World War

"Destroy!" rings out the battle cry at level 5. It's not enough that one wins; others must lose. "We must make sure this horrible situation does not happen again!" Only one option at level 5 exists: to separate the combatants (aka team members) so that they don't hurt one another. No constructive outcome can be had.

http://agile.dzone.com/articles/agile-managing-conflict

Conflict Types	**#1 - Lack of Role Clarity** The project manager is responsible for assigning tasks to each project team member. In addition, they often assume that team members understand what is being asked of them. This assumption can be incorrect, leading to team members being unclear on what needs to be accomplished. A good project manager takes the time to explain the tasks, their expectations and timeframes around completion. **#2 - Difference in Prioritizing Tasks** Just because the project manager thinks the task is a milestone, the team member completing the task may not. Team members may be working simultaneously on multiple projects and cannot differentiate the priority of one project's tasks from another. The project manager should try to explain the importance of the overall project to the **#3 - Working in Silos** Often, project team members work independently. They may work remotely or in a different location from other project team members. Conflict arises when team members are not aware of what others are doing and are not communicating with one another. The project manager needs to bring the team together to discuss project status and barriers to getting the project completed promptly. If team members working in silos can envision how they are a part of the bigger picture, they will be more motivated and feel like a part of the team. **#4 - Lack of Communication** Project managers must foster a clear line of communication between project team members. In order to minimize duplication of efforts, the project manager should communicate expectations

	to all team members. The project manager needs to be easily accessible to project team members at all times during the project. If team members cannot reach their project manager or other team members, they may spin in circles needlessly. **# 5 - Waiting on Completion of Task Dependencies** Some tasks cannot be started until other tasks are completed. Team members need to understand the impact of their role on others. For example if one team member is responsible for ordering equipment and another for installing the equipment, one task is dependent on the other. Conflict can occur if the first team member is delayed in completing their tasks. http://www.brighthub.com/office/project-management/articles/95971.aspx
Container	A container is a closed space where things can get done, regardless of the overall complexity of the problem. In the case of Scrum, a container is a Sprint, an iteration. We put people with all the skills needed to solve the problem in the container. We put the highest value problems to be solved into the container. Then we protect the container from any outside disturbances while the people attempt to bring the problem to a solution. We control the container by time-boxing the length of time that we allow the problem to be worked on. We let the people select problems of a size that can be brought to fruition during the time-box. At the end of the time-box, we open the container and inspect the results. We then reset the container (adaptation) for the next time-box. By frequently replanning and shifting our work, we are able to optimize value. http://kenschwaber.wordpress.com/2010/06/10/waterfall-leankanban-and-scrum-2/
Continuous Integration	Continuous Integration (CI) involves producing a clean build of the system several times per day. Agile teams typically configure CI to include automated compilation, unit test execution, and source control integration. Sometimes CI also includes automatically running automated acceptance tests. **Continuous Integration Technique, Tools, and Policy** There are several specific practices that CI seems to require to work well. On his site, Martin Fowler provides a long, detailed description of what Continuous Integration is and how to make it work. One popular CI rule states that programmers never leave anything unintegrated at the end of the day. The build should never spend the night in a broken state. This imposes some task planning discipline on programming teams. Furthermore, if the team's rule is that whoever breaks the build at check-in has to fix it again, there is a natural incentive to check code in frequently during the day. **Benefits of Continuous Integration** When CI works well, it helps the code stay robust enough that customers and other stakeholders can play with the code whenever they like. This speeds the flow of development work overall; as Fowler points out, it has a very different feel to it. It also encourages more feedback between programmers and customers, which helps the team get things right before iteration deadlines. Like refactoring, continuous integration works well if you have an exhaustive suite of automated unit tests that ensure that you are not committing buggy code. http://www.versionone.com/Agile101/Continuous_Integration.asp http://www.martinfowler.com/articles/continuousIntegration.html
Control Limits	Control limits, also known as natural process limits, are horizontal lines drawn on a statistical process control chart, usually at a distance of ±3 standard deviations of the plotted statistic from the statistic's mean. Used in Agile Control charts

	https://en.wikipedia.org/wiki/Control_limits
Cumulative Flow Diagrams	The Cumulative Flow diagram is very similar to a Burnup Chart. It shows how much of our work (i.e., the effort associated with User Stories) is in different states, such as Completed or In Progress. The Total and Completed curves shows the Release scope and Burnup of completed work, while the In Progress curve shows how much work is associated with Stories currently in development. The primary difference from the standard Burnup and Cumulative Flow diagrams is that the latter shows how much of the work is currently in progress. https://www.cprime.com/resource/templates/cumulative-flow-diagram-burnup-chart/
Customer-Valued Prioritization	Agile development is about the frequent delivery of high-value, working software to the customer/user community. Doing so requires the prioritization of user stories and the continuous monitoring of the prioritized story backlog. The primary driver for prioritization is customer value. However, it is insufficient to simply say that the highest-value stories are the highest priority. Product owners must also factor in the cost of development. An extremely valuable feature quickly loses its luster when it is also extremely costly to implement. Additionally, there are other secondary drivers such as risk and uncertainty. These should be resolved early. There may also be experimental stories that are worth developing early to find out whether customers see value in further development along those lines. There may be other prioritization drivers, but business value should always be foremost. 1. Complete the high-value, high-risk stories first if the cost is justified. 2. Complete the high-value, low-risk stories next if the cost is justified. 3. Complete the lower-value, low-risk stories next. 4. Avoid low-value, high-risk stories. http://www.scribd.com/doc/111905434/Agile-Analytics-a-Value-Driven-Approach-Ken-Collier
Cycle Time	Cycle time for software development is measured in the number of days needed between feature specification and production delivery. This is called: Software In Process (SIP). A shorter cycle indicates a healthier project. A Lean project that deploys to production every 2-weeks has a SIP of 10 working days. Some Lean projects even deploy nightly. https://jaymeedwards.com/2012/04/09/cycle-time-the-important-statistic-you-probably-arent-measuring/

Daily Scrums/Daily Stand-Ups	Time-boxed 15 minutes meetings whose purpose is the providing of a concise team status. Scrum has each team member asked by the ScrumMaster the following questions: • What did you do yesterday? • What are you doing today? • Are there any impediments that need resolution? (EXAM TIP: I had a couple of questions relating to the purpose of this meeting) http://www.mountaingoatsoftware.com/scrum/daily-scrum
Declaration Of Interdependence	The **PM Declaration of interdependence** is a set of six management principles initially intended for project managers of Agile Software Development projects We are a community of project leaders that are highly successful at delivering results. To achieve these results: ▪ We **increase return on investment** by making continuous flow of value our focus. ▪ We **deliver reliable results** by engaging customers in frequent interactions and shared ownership. ▪ We **expect uncertainty** and manage for it through iterations, anticipation, and adaptation. ▪ We **unleash creativity and innovation** by recognizing that individuals are the ultimate source of value, and creating an environment where they can make a difference. ▪ We **boost performance** through group accountability for results and shared responsibility for team effectiveness. ▪ We **improve effectiveness and reliability** through situationally specific strategies, processes and practices. http://pmdoi.org/
D.E.E.P.	• **Detailed Appropriately.** User stories on the product backlog that will be done soon need to be sufficiently well understood that they can be completed in the coming sprint. Stories that will not be developed for awhile should be described with less detail. • **Estimated.** The product backlog is more than a list of all work to be done; it is also a useful planning tool. Because items further down the backlog are not as well understood (yet), the estimates associated with them will be less precise than estimates given items at the top. • **Emergent.** A product backlog is not static. It will change over time. As more is learned, user stories on the product backlog will be added, removed, or reprioritized. • **Prioritized.** The product backlog should be sorted with the most valuable items at the top and the least valuable at the bottom. By always working in priority order, the team is able to maximize the value of the product or system being developed. http://www.mountaingoatsoftware.com/blog/make-the-product-backlog-deep
Definition Of Done	Definition of Done (DoD) is a simple list of activities (writing code, coding comments, unit testing, integration testing, release notes, design documents, etc.) that add verifiable/demonstrable value to the product. Focusing on value-added steps allows the team to focus on what must be completed in order to build software while eliminating wasteful activities that only complicate software development efforts. Note – the DoD is defined by the Product Owner and committed to by the team. http://www.scrumalliance.org/articles/105-what-is-definition-of-done-dod

Defect Rate	The defect detection rate is the amount of defects detected per sprint. Assuming that developers produce defects at a more or less constant rate, it is correlated with the velocity; the more story points are delivered, the more defects should be found and fixed as well. Teams tend to be pretty consistent in the quality of the software they deliver, so a drop in velocity combined with a rise in the defect detection rate should trigger the alarm. Something's cooking and you need to find out what it is. My personal opinion is that a lower defect detection rate isn't necessarily better than a higher one. A defect more found in one of the development and test environments is a defect less that makes it into production. From that perspective, you could support the statement, the more defects the better. http://theagileprojectmanager.blogspot.com/2013/05/agile-metrics.html
Discounted Pay-Back Period	A capital budgeting procedure used to determine the profitability of a project. In contrast to an NPV analysis, which provides the overall value of a project, a discounted payback period gives the number of years it takes to break even from undertaking the initial expenditure. Future cash flows are considered are discounted to time "zero." This procedure is similar to a payback period; however, the discounted payback period measures how long it take for the initial cash outflow to be paid back, including the time value of money. http://accountingexplained.com/managerial/capital-budgeting/discounted-payback-period

Dreyfus Model of Skill Acquisition	**1. Novice**
	   • "rigid adherence to taught rules or plans"
	   • no exercise of "discretionary judgment"
	2. Advanced beginner
	   • limited "situational perception"
	   • all aspects of work treated separately with equal importance
	3. Competent
	   • "coping with crowdedness" (multiple activities, accumulation of information)
	   • some perception of actions in relation to goals
	   • deliberate planning
	   • formulates routines
	4. Proficient
	   • holistic view of situation
	   • prioritizes importance of aspects
	   • "perceives deviations from the normal pattern"
	   • employs maxims for guidance, with meanings that adapt to the situation at hand
	5. Expert
	   • transcends reliance on rules, guidelines, and maxims
	   • "intuitive grasp of situations based on deep, tacit understanding"
	   • has "vision of what is possible"
	   • uses "analytical approaches" in new situations or in case of problems
	
	https://en.wikipedia.org/wiki/Dreyfus_model_of_skill_acquisition

DRY	Software must be written expecting for future change. Principles like **D**on't **R**epeat **Y**ourself (DRY) are used to facilitate this. In agile development, changes to the software specifications are welcome even in late stages of development. As clients get more hands-on time with iterative builds of the software, they may be able to better communicate their needs. Also, changes in the market or company structure might dictate changes in the software specifications. Agile development is designed to accommodate these late changes.

	https://code.tutsplus.com/tutorials/3-key-software-principles-you-must-understand--net-25161
Earned Value Management (EVM)	Agile EVM is now all about executing the project and tracking the accumulated EV according to the simple earning rule. Because Agile EVM has been evolving for many years the following practices are well-established: • EV is accumulated at fixed time intervals (i.e. Timebox, Iteration or Sprint) of 1–4 weeks; • PV and EV is graphically tracked & extrapolated as remaining value in a Release Burndown Chart as shown in figure 6; • Rather than a S-shaped curve the PV in Agile EVM is a straight line because an Agile project has no distinct phases and corresponding variances in the rate of value delivery; • The EV in Story Points done in one fixed time interval is known as the Velocity of a team; • In Agile scope change is embraced and the amount of added (removed) scope in Story Points is added (removed) to the Velocity or Scope Floor. The latter is shown in Figure 6 where several scope increases have lowered the Scope Floor below the x-axis. The advantage of using a Scope Floor is that any scope changes can easily be separated from Velocity variances; • The intersection between the Remaining Value and Scope Floor lines indicates the expected release date and the corresponding Remaining Budget. (EXAM TIP –There was a question on the exam that asked when was the best time to measure EVM) http://en.wikipedia.org/wiki/Earned_value_management#Agile_EVM
Emotional Intelligence	**Self Awareness** Awareness of one's own feelings and the ability to recognize and manage these feelings in a way which one feels that one can control. This factor includes a degree of self-belief in one's ability to manage one's emotions and to control their impact in a work environment. **Emotional Resilience** The ability to perform consistently in a range of situations under pressure and to adapt one's behavior appropriately. The facility to balance the needs and concerns of the individuals involved. The ability to retain focus on a course of action or need for results in the face of personal challenge or criticism. **Motivation** The drive and energy to achieve clear results and make an impact: and to balance both short and long term goals with an ability to pursue demanding goals in the face of rejection or questioning. **Interpersonal Sensitivity** The facility to be aware of, and take account of, the needs and perceptions of others when arriving at decisions and proposing solutions to problems and challenges. The ability to build from this awareness and achieve 'buy-in' to decisions and ideas for action. **Influence** The ability to persuade others to change a viewpoint based on the understanding of the position and the recognition of the need to listen to this perspective and provide a rationale for change. **Intuitiveness** The ability to arrive at clear decisions and drive their implementation when presented with incomplete or ambiguous information using both rational and 'emotional' or insightful perceptions of key issues and implications. **Conscientiousness** The ability to display clear commitment to a course of action in the face of challenge and to match 'words and deeds'; in encouraging others to support the chosen direction. The personal

	commitment to pursuing an ethical solution to a difficult business issue or problem. http://businessagile.blogspot.com/2005/02/emotional-intelligence-key-element-of.html
Empirical Process Control	**Empirical Process Control** The word "empirical" denotes information gained by means of observation, experience, or experiment. The empirical process control constitutes a continuous cycle of inspecting the process for correct operation and results and adapting the process as needed. There are three legs that hold up every implementation of empirical process control: **transparency, inspection, and adaptation**. The first leg is transparency. It means that those aspects of the process that affect the outcome must be visible to those controlling the process. The second leg is inspection. The various aspects of the process must be inspected frequently enough that unacceptable variances in the process can be detected. The third leg of empirical process control is adaptation. The process or the material being processed must be adjusted if one or more aspects of the process are outside acceptable limits and the resulting product will be unacceptable. http://www.scrumstudy.com/scrum-empirical-process-control.asp
Escaped Defects	Escaped Defects are those defects reported by the Customer that have escaped all software quality processes are represented in this metric. Escaping defects should then be treated as ranked backlog work items, along with other project work items. They should be prioritized high enough to resolve them within the next sprint or two and not accumulate a growing backlog. Watch the defect backlog as part of the project metrics. A growing defect backlog is a key indicator that the team is taking on more new work than it can handle. It may also be a key indicator that the team is operating as a "mini-waterfall" project, rather than a agile project, requiring more collaboration between Dev and Quality Engineers and early testing. Drop the number of new items the team works on until the escaping defects are well managed or eliminated. http://qablog.practitest.com/process-quality-feedback-and-escaping-defects/
Exploratory Testing	Exploratory Testing is a technique for finding surprising defects. Testers use their training, experience, and intuition to form hypotheses about where defects are likely to be lurking in the software, then they use a fast feedback loop to iteratively generate, execute, and refine test plans that expose those defects. It appears similar to ad-hoc testing to an untrained observer, but it's far more rigorous. Some teams use exploratory testing to check the quality of their software. After a story's been coded, the testers do some exploratory testing, the team fixes bugs, and repeat. Once the testers don't find any more bugs, the story is done. (EXAM TIP: This is also referred to as testing performed between Done and Done-Done) http://jamesshore.com/Blog/Alternatives-to-Acceptance-Testing.html
Extreme Programming	Extreme Programming (or XP) is a set of values, principles and practices for rapidly developing high-quality software that provides the highest value for the customer in the fastest way possible. XP is extreme in the sense that it takes 12 well-known software development "best practices" to their logical extremes. The 12 core practices of XP are:

	1) **The Planning Game**: Business and development cooperate to produce the maximum business value as rapidly as possible. The planning game happens at various scales, but the basic rules are always the same:
	   a) Business comes up with a list of desired features for the system. Each feature is written out as a **User Story**, which gives the feature a name, and describes in broad strokes what is required. User stories are typically written on 4x6 cards.
	   b) Development estimates how much effort each story will take, and how much effort the team can produce in a given time interval (the iteration).
	   c) Business then decides which stories to implement in what order, as well as when and how often to produce a production releases of the system.
	2) **Small Releases**: Start with the smallest useful feature set. Release early and often, adding a few features each time.
	3) **System Metaphor**: Each project has an organizing metaphor, which provides an easy to remember naming convention.
	4) **Simple Design**: Always use the simplest possible design that gets the job done. The requirements will change tomorrow, so only do what's needed to meet today's requirements.
	5) **Continuous Testing**: Before programmers add a feature, they write a test for it. When the suite runs, the job is done. Tests in XP come in two basic flavors.
	   a) **Unit Tests** are automated tests written by the developers to test functionality as they write it. Each unit test typically tests only a single class, or a small cluster of classes. Unit tests are typically written using a unit testing framework, such as JUnit.
	   b) **Acceptance Tests** (also known as **Functional Tests**) are specified by the customer to test that the overall system is functioning as specified. Acceptance tests typically test the entire system, or some large chunk of it. When all the acceptance tests pass for a given user story, that story is considered complete. At the very least, an acceptance test could consist of a script of user interface actions and expected results that a human can run. Ideally acceptance tests should be automated, either using the unit testing framework, or a separate acceptance testing framework.
	6) **Refactoring**: Refactor out any duplicate code generated in a coding session. You can do this with confidence that you didn't break anything because you have the tests.
	7) **Pair Programming**: All production code is written by two programmers sitting at one machine. Essentially, all code is reviewed as it is written.
	8) **Collective Code Ownership**: No single person "owns" a module. Any developer is expect to be able to work on any part of the codebase at any time.
	9) **Continuous Integration**: All changes are integrated into the codebase at least daily. The tests have to run 100% both before and after integration.
	10) **40-Hour Work Week**: Programmers go home on time. In crunch mode, up to one week of overtime is allowed. But multiple consecutive weeks of overtime are treated as a sign that something is very wrong with the process.
	11) **On-site Customer**: Development team has continuous access to a real live customer, that is, someone who will actually be using the system. For commercial software with lots of customers, a customer proxy (usually the product manager) is used instead.
	12) **Coding Standards**: Everyone codes to the same standards. Ideally, you shouldn't be able to tell by looking at it who on the team has touched a specific piece of code.
	
	(EXAM TIP: Lots of questions about Lean, XP and Scrum principles)
	
	http://www.jera.com/techinfo/xpfaq.html

Feature	During detailed planning, agile development favors a feature breakdown structure (FBS)

Breakdown Structure (FBS)	approach instead of the work breakdown structure (WBS) used in waterfall development approaches. Feature breakdown structures are advantageous for a few reasons: 1. They allow communication between the customer and the development team in terms both can understand. 2. They allow the customer to prioritize the team's work based on business value. 3. They allow tracking of work against the actual business value produced. It is acceptable to start out with features that are large and then break them out into smaller features over time. This allows the customer to keep from diving in to too much detail until that detail is needed to help facilitate actual design and delivery. http://www.versionone.com/agile-101/agile-feature-estimation/
Fishbone diagram	The fishbone diagram identifies many possible causes for an effect or problem. It can be used to structure a brainstorming session. It immediately sorts ideas into useful categories. http://asq.org/learn-about-quality/cause-analysis-tools/overview/fishbone.html
The Five Whys	A technique for identifying the exact root cause of a problem to determine the appropriate solution. Made popular in the 70s by the Toyota Production System, the 5 whys is a flexible problem solving technique. http://businessanalystlearnings.com/ba-techniques/2013/2/5/root-cause-analysis-the-5-whys-technique
Fractional Assignments	All of the team members should sit with the team full-time and give the project their complete attention. This particularly applies to customers, who are often surprised at the level of involvement XP requires of them. Some organizations like to assign people to multiple projects simultaneously. This fractional assignment is particularly common in matrix-managed organizations. (If team members have two managers, one for their project and one for their function, you're probably in a matrixed organization.) Fractional assignment is dreadfully counterproductive. If your company practices fractional assignment, I have some good news. You can instantly improve productivity by reassigning people to only one project at a time. Fractional assignment is dreadfully counterproductive: fractional workers don't bond with their teams; they often aren't around to hear conversations and answer questions and they must task switch, which incurs a significant hidden penalty. "The minimum penalty is 15 percent... Fragmented knowledge workers may look busy, but a lot of their busyness is just thrashing." [DeMarco 2002] (p.19-20) That's not to say that everyone needs to work with the team for the entire duration of the project. You can bring someone in to consult on a problem temporarily. However, while she works with the team, she should be fully engaged and available. http://www.jamesshore.com/Agile-Book/the_xp_team.html Tom DeMarco and Barry Boehm. 2002. The Agile Methods Fray. *Computer* 35, 6 (June 2002)
Frequent Verification And Validation	The terms Verification and Validation are commonly used in software engineering to mean two different types of analysis. The usual definitions are: **Validation**: Are we building the right system? **Verification**: Are we building the system right? In other words, validation is concerned with checking that the system will meet the customer's

	actual needs, while verification is concerned with whether the system is well-engineered, error-free, and so on. Verification will help to determine whether the software is of high quality, but it will not ensure that the system is useful. The distinction between the two terms is largely to do with the role of specifications. Validation is the process of checking whether the specification captures the customer's needs, while verification is the process of checking that the software meets the specification. Verification includes all the activities associated with the producing high quality software: testing, inspection, design analysis, specification analysis, and so on. It is a relatively objective process, in that if the various products and documents are expressed precisely enough, no subjective judgements should be needed in order to verify software. http://www.easterbrook.ca/steve/2010/11/the-difference-between-verification-and-validation/
Ideal Time	Like Work Units, Ideal Time excludes non-programming time. When a team uses Ideal Time for estimating, they are referring explicitly to only the programmer time required to get a feature or task done, compared to other features or tasks. Again, during the first few iterations, estimate history accumulates, a real velocity emerges, and Ideal Time can be mapped to real, elapsed time. Many teams using Ideal Time have found that their ultimate effort exceeds initial programmer estimates by 1-2x, and that this stabilizes, within an acceptable range, over a few iterations. On a task by task basis the ratio will vary, but over an entire iteration, the ratios that teams develop have proven to remain pretty consistent. For a given team, a known historical ratio of Ideal Time to real time can be especially valuable in planning releases. A team may quickly look at the required functionality and provide a high level estimate of 200 ideal days. If the team's historical ratio of ideal to real is about 2.5, the team may feel fairly confident in submitting an estimate of 500 project days. In fixed-bid scenarios, this kind of estimate can be reliable. https://www.versionone.com/agile-101/agile-management-practices/agile-feature-estimation/
Information Radiator	An information radiator is a large display of critical team information that is continuously updated and located in a spot where the team can see it constantly. The term "information radiator" was introduced extensively with a solid theoretical framework in Agile Software Development by Alistair Cockburn. Information radiators are typically used to display the state of work packages, the condition of tests or the progress of the team. Team members are usually free to update the information radiator. Some information radiators may have rules about how they are updated. Whiteboards, flip charts, poster boards or large electronic displays can all be used as the base media for an information radiator. For teams new to adopting agile work practices the best medium is usually a poster board on the wall with index cards and push pins. The index cards have a small amount of information on each of them and the push pins allow them to be moved around. Information radiators help amplify feedback, empower teams and focus a team on work results. Too many information radiators become confusing to understand and cumbersome to maintain. If an information radiator is not being updated it should be reconsidered and either changed or discarded. Robert McGeachy recommended a list of information radiators to be a part of every team room. Apart from the standard Scrum Artifacts, his list included,

	<ul><li>Team structure with who's on the team</li><li>Client Organization structure</li><li>High Level and Mid Level plans</li><li>Client Phase exit criteria</li><li>Team performance survey results</li><li>Risks</li><li>Recognition awards</li><li>Ground Rules</li></ul> http://www.agileadvice.com/archives/2005/05/information_rad.html
Internal Rate Of Return (IRR)	Internal rates of return are commonly used to evaluate the desirability of investments or projects. The higher a project's internal rate of return, the more desirable it is to undertake the project. Assuming all projects require the same amount of up-front investment, the project with the highest IRR would be considered the best and undertaken first. A firm (or individual) should, in theory, undertake all projects or investments available with IRRs that exceed the cost of capital. Investment may be limited by availability of funds to the firm and/or by the firm's capacity or ability to manage numerous projects. In more specific terms, the IRR of an investment is the discount rate at which the net present value of costs (negative cash flows) of the investment equals the net present value of the benefits (positive cash flows) of the investment. http://en.wikipedia.org/wiki/Internal_rate_of_return
Iteration And Release Planning	Release planning is the process of transforming a product vision into a product backlog. The release plan is the visible and estimated product backlog itself, overlaid with the measured velocity of the delivery organization; it provides visual controls and a roadmap with predictable release points. http://www.netobjectives.com/files/Lean-AgileReleasePlanning.pdf
I.N.V.E.S.T.	Attributes of an effective user story: <table><tr><td>Independent</td><td>The user story should be self-contained, in a way that there is no inherent dependency on another user story.</td></tr><tr><td>Negotiable</td><td>User stories, up until they are part of a Sprint, can always be changed and rewritten.</td></tr><tr><td>Valuable</td><td>A user story must deliver value to the end user.</td></tr><tr><td>Estimable</td><td>You must always be able to estimate the size of a user story.</td></tr><tr><td>Sized appropriately or Small</td><td>User stories should not be so big as to become impossible to plan/task/prioritize with a certain level of certainty.</td></tr><tr><td>Testable</td><td>The user story or its related description must provide the necessary information to make test development</td></tr></table> http://www.agileforall.com/2009/05/new-to-agile-invest-in-good-user-stories/
Kaizen	Kaizen is the practice of continuous improvement. Kaizen was originally introduced to the West by Masaaki Imai in his book Kaizen: The Key to Japan's Competitive Success in 1986. Today Kaizen is recognized worldwide as an important pillar of an organization's long-term competitive

	strategy. http://www.kaizen.com/about-us/definition-of-kaizen.html
Kanban Boards	A Kanban means a ticket describing a task to do. A Kanban Board shows the current status of all the tasks to be done within this iteration. The tasks are represented by cards (Post-It Notes), and the statuses are presented by areas on the board separated and labeled with the status. This Kanban Board helps the team understand how they are doing well as well as what to do next and makes the team self-directing. 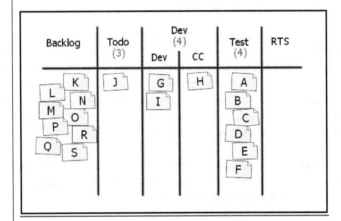 http://www.infoq.com/articles/agile-kanban-boards http://blog.brodzinski.com/2009/11/kanban-story-kanban-board.html
Kano Model	The Kano model offers some insight into the product attributes which are perceived to be important to customers. The purpose of the tool is to support product specification and discussion through better development team understanding. Kano's model focuses on differentiating product features, as opposed to focusing initially on customer needs. Kano also produced a methodology for mapping consumer responses to questionnaires onto his model. The model involves two dimensions: • Achievement (the horizontal axis) which runs from *the supplier didn't do it at all* to *the supplier did it very well*. • Satisfaction (the vertical axis) that goes from *total dissatisfaction* with the product or service to *total satisfaction* with the product or service. Dr. Noriaki Kano isolated and identified three levels of customer expectations: that is, what it takes to positively impact customer satisfaction. The figure below portrays the three levels of need: expected, normal, and exciting. **Expected Needs** Fully satisfying the customer at this level simply gets a supplier into the market. The entry level expectations are the *must* level qualities, properties, or attributes. These expectations are also known as the *dissatisfiers* because by themselves they cannot fully satisfy a customer. However, failure to provide these basic expectations will cause dissatisfaction. Examples include attributes relative to safety, latest generation automotive components such as a self-starter, and the use of all new parts if a product is offered for sale as previously unused or new. The *musts* include customer assumptions, expected qualities, expected functions, and other *unspoken* expectations. **Normal Needs** These are the qualities, attributes, and characteristics that keep a supplier in the market. These next higher level expectations are known as the *wants* or the *satisfiers* because they are the ones that customers will specify as though from a list. They can either satisfy or

	dissatisfy the customer depending on their presence or absence. The *wants* include *voice of the customer* requirements and other *spoken* expectations (see table below). **Exciting Needs** The highest level of customer expectations, as described by Kano, is termed the *wow* level qualities, properties, or attributes. These expectations are also known as the *delighters* or *exciters* because they go well beyond anything the customer might imagine and ask for. Their absence does nothing to hurt a possible sale, but their presence improves the likelihood of purchase. *Wows* not only excite customers to make on-the-spot purchases but make them return for future purchases. These are *unspoken* ways of knocking the customer's socks off. Examples include heads-up display in a front windshield, forward- and rear-facing radars, and a 100,000 mile warranty. Over time, as demonstrated by the arrow going from top left to bottom right in the Kano model, *wows* become *wants* become *musts*, as in, for example, automobile self-starters and automatic transmissions. 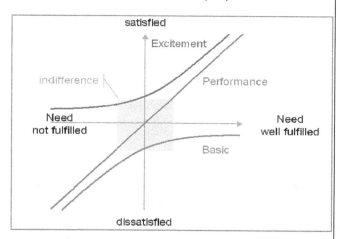 http://asq.org/learn-about-quality/qfd-quality-function-deployment/overview/kano-model.html http://en.wikipedia.org/wiki/Kano_model
KPIs in Agile	1. **Actual Stories Completed vs. Committed Stories** – the team's ability to understand and predict its capabilities. To measure, compare the number of stories committed to in sprint planning with the stories identified as completed in the sprint review. 2. **Technical Debt Management** – the known problems and issues delivered at the end of the sprint. It is usually measured by the number of bugs, but may also include deliverables such as training material, user documentation and delivery media. 3. **Team Velocity** – the consistency of the team's estimates from sprint to sprint. Calculate by comparing story points completed in the current sprint with points completed in the previous sprint; aim for +/- 10 percent. 4. **Quality Delivered to Customers** – Are we building the product the customer needs? Does every sprint provide value to customers and become a potentially releasable piece of the product? It's not necessarily a product ready to release but rather a work in progress, designed to solicit customer comments, opinions and suggestions. This can best be measured by surveying the customers and stakeholders. 5. **Team Enthusiasm** – a major component for a successful scrum team. If teammates aren't enthusiastic, no process or methodology will help. Measuring enthusiasm can be done by observing various sprint meetings or, the most straightforward approach, simply asking team members "Do you feel happy?" and "How motivated do you feel?" 6. **Retrospective Process Improvement** – the scrum team's ability to revise its development process to make it more effective and enjoyable for the next sprint. This can be measured using the count of retrospective items identified, the retrospective items the team committed to addressing and the items resolved by the end of the sprint. 7. **Communication** – how well the team, product owner, scrum master, customers and stakeholders are conducting open and honest communications. Through observing and listening you will get indications and clues about how well everyone is communicating.

	8. **Team's Adherence to Scrum Rules and Engineering Practices** – Although scrum doesn't prescribe engineering practices—unlike XP—most companies define several of their own for their projects. You want to ensure that the scrum team follows the rules your company defines. This can be measured by counting the infractions that occur during each sprint. 9. **Team's Understanding of Sprint Scope and Goal** – a subjective measure of how well the customer, product team and development team understand and focus on the sprint stories and goal. The goal is usually aligned with the intended customer value to be delivered and is defined in the acceptance criteria of the stories. This is best determined through day-to-day contact and interaction with the team and customer feedback. http://pragmaticmarketing.com/resources/9-scrum-metrics-to-keep-your-team-on-track
Lead Time	Lead time is a term borrowed from the manufacturing method known as Lean or Toyota Production System, where it is defined as the time elapsed between a customer placing an order and receiving the product ordered. http://guide.agilealliance.org/guide/leadtime.html

Lean Development	Lean software development is a translation of lean manufacturing and lean IT principles and practices to the software development domain.
	1. **Eliminate Waste**
	    • Provide market and technical leadership - your company can be successful by producing innovative and technologically advanced products but you must understand what your customers value and you know what technology you're using can deliver
	    • Create nothing but value - you have to be careful with all the processes you follow i.e. be sure that all of them are required and they are focused on creating value
	    • Write less code - the more code you have the more tests you need thus it requires more work and if you're writing tests for features that are not needed you are simply wasting time
	2. **Create Knowledge**
	    • Create design-build teams - leader of the development team has to listen to his/her members and ask smart questions encouraging them to look for the answers and to get back with encountered problems or invented solutions as soon as possible
	    • Maintain a culture of constant improvement - create environment in which people will be constantly improving what they are working on - they should know that they are not and should not be perfect - they always have a field to improve and they should do it
	    • Teach problem-solving methods - development team should behave like small research institute, they should establish hypotheses and conduct many rapid experiments in order to verify them
	3. **Build Quality In**
	    • Synchronize - in order to achieve high quality in your software you should start worrying about it before you write single line of working code - don't wait with synchronization because it will hurt
	    • Automate - automate testing, building, installations, anything that is routine, but do it smartly, do it in a way people can improve the process and change anything they want without worrying that after the change is done the software will stop working
	    • Refactor - eliminate code duplication to ZERO - every time it shows up refactor the code, the tests, and the documentation to minimize the complexity
	4. **Defer Commitment**

- Schedule Irreversible Decisions at the Last Responsible Moment - you should know where you want to go but you don't know the road very well, you will be discovering it day after day - the most important thing is to keep the right direction
- Break Dependencies - components should be coupled as loosely as possible to enable implementation in any order
- Maintain Options - develop multiple solutions for all critical decisions and see which one works best

5. **Optimize the Whole**
   - Focus on the Entire Value Stream - focus on winning the whole race which is the software - don't optimize local inefficiencies, see the whole and optimize the whole organization
   - Deliver a Complete Product - teams need to have great leaders as well as great engineers, sales, marketing specialists, secretaries, etc. - they together can deliver great final products to their customers

6. **Deliver Fast**
   - Work in small batches - reduce projects size, shorten release cycles, stabilize work environment (listen to what your velocity tells you), repeat what's good and eradicate practices that creates obstacles
   - Limit work to capacity - limit tasks queue to minimum (one or two iterations ahead is enough), don't be afraid of removing items from the queue - reject any work until you have an empty slot in your queue
   - Focus on cycle time, not utilization - put in your queue small tasks that cannot clog the process for a long time - reduce cycle time and have fewer things to process in your queue

7. **Respect People**
   - Train team leaders/supervisors - give team leaders the training, the guidance and some free space to implement lean thinking in their environment
   - Move responsibility and decision making to the lowest possible level - let your people think and decide on their own - they know better how to implement difficult algorithms and apply state-of-the-art software frameworks
   - Foster pride in workmanship - encourage passionate involvement of your team members to what and how they do

(EXAM TIP: Lots of questions about Lean, XP and Scrum principles)

http://www.disciplinedagiledelivery.com/lean-principles/

Learning Cycles	The Build–Measure–Learn loop emphasizes speed as a critical ingredient to product development. A team or company's effectiveness is determined by its ability to ideate, quickly build a minimum viable product of that idea, measure its effectiveness in the market, and learn from that experiment. In other words, it's a learning cycle of turning ideas into products, measuring customers' reactions and behaviors against built products, and then deciding whether to persevere or pivot the idea; this process repeats as many times as necessary. The phases of the loop are: Ideas –> Build –> Product –> Measure –> Data –> Learn https://en.wikipedia.org/wiki/Lean_startup
Minimally Marketable Feature (MMF)	Start by identifying your product's most desirable features. Prioritize their value, either through a formal technique or by subjectively ranking each one against the others. Once you've done so, plan your releases around the features. Release the highest-value features first to maximize their return. To accelerate delivery, have your entire team collaborate on one feature at a time and perform releases as often as possible.

	http://jamesshore.com/Articles/Business/Software%20Profitability%20Newsletter/Phased%20Releases.html
Minimal Viable Product (MVP)	A Minimum Viable Product is that version of a new product which allows a team to collect the maximum amount of validated learning about customers with the least effort. http://leanstack.com/minimum-viable-product/
MoSCoW	The MoSCoW approach to prioritization originated from the DSDM methodology (Dynamic Software Development Method), which was possibly the first agile methodology (?) – even before we knew iterative development as 'agile'. MoSCoW is a fairly simple way to sort features (or user stories) into priority order – a way to help teams quickly understand the customer's view of what is essential for launch and what is not. MoSCoW stands for: • **M**ust have (or Minimum Usable Subset) • **S**hould have • **C**ould have • **W**on't have (but Would like in future) http://www.allaboutagile.com/prioritization-using-moscow/
Multistage Integration Builds	Multi-stage Continuous Integration (MSCI) is an extension of the common practice of shielding others from additional changes by only checking-in when individual changes have been tested and only updating an individual workspace when it's ready to absorb other people's changes. With MSCI, each team does a team-based continuous integration first and then cross-integrates the team's changes with the mainline on success. This limits project-wide churn and allows continuous integration to scale to large projects. https://en.wikipedia.org/wiki/Multi-stage_continuous_integration
Net Present Value (NPV)	The difference between the present value of cash inflows and the present value of cash outflows. NPV is used in capital budgeting to analyze the profitability of an investment or project. NPV compares the value of a dollar today to the value of that same dollar in the future, taking inflation and returns into account. If the NPV of a prospective project is positive, it should be accepted. However, if NPV is negative, the project should probably be rejected because cash flows will also be negative. **Formula** Each cash inflow/outflow is discounted back to its present value (PV). Then they are summed. Therefore NPV is the sum of all terms, $$\frac{R_t}{(1+i)^t}$$ where t - the time of the cash flow i - the discount rate (the rate of return that could be earned on an investment in the financial markets with similar risk.); the opportunity cost of capital R_t - the net cash flow (the amount of cash, inflow minus outflow) at time t. For

	educational purposes, R_0 is commonly placed to the left of the sum to emphasize its role as (minus) the investment. http://en.wikipedia.org/wiki/Net_present_value
Negotiation	Negotiation, meaning "discussion intended to produce agreement", is fundamental to every software project. (And other projects too – my examples just happen to come from the software industry.) Developers and customers must reach agreement on what the system is supposed to do. A wise agreement will define achievable goals and meet the users' real needs. In Fisher and Ury's book, *Getting to Yes,* they call their approach "principled negotiation". It contains four key elements: • Separate People from the Problem • Focus on Interests, not Positions • Invent Options for Mutual Gain • Use Objective Criteria Both parties would be better served to engage in dialog about their underlying interests. Such dialog is encouraged by agile processes. They promote discussion, provide better opportunities to explore interests, and avoid premature "lock in" of positions. Fisher and Ury's style of negotiation is not about winning and losing. It's about *everybody winning*. http://www.agilekiwi.com/peopleskills/the-power-of-negotiation/ Fisher, Roger and William Ury. Getting to Yes: Negotiating Agreement Without Giving In. New York, NY: Penguin Books, 1983.
Open Space Meetings	**Opening**: 1. Show the timeline (agenda), how the event breaks down into Opening, Marketplace of ideas, Break-out sessions, Closing. 2. Sponsor introduces the theme. Briefly. One or two minutes max. Long openings drain the energy of the meeting quickly. Get participants to work ASAP. 3. Facilitators introduce the principles and the format. Explain how the marketplace of ideas works. **Marketplace of ideas**: 1. Participants write 'issues' on pieces of paper. Preferably with bold markers, so they are easy to read from a distance. 2. Participants choose a timeslot for their topic on the agenda wall. 3. One by one, participants explain their issue to the others, with the aim of drawing the right people to their break-out-session. http://www.chriscorrigan.com/parkinglot/planning-an-open-space-technology-meeting/
Osmotic Communications	Osmotic communication means that information flows into the background hearing of members of the team, so that they pick up relevant information as though by osmosis. This is normally accomplished by seating them in the same room. Then, when one person asks a question, others in the room can either tune in or tune out, contributing to the discussion or continuing with their work. When osmotic communication is in place, questions and answers flow naturally and with surprisingly little disturbance among the team. http://alistair.cockburn.us/Osmotic+communication
Pareto Principle	Pareto's law is more commonly known as the 80/20 rule. The theory is about the law of

	distribution and how many things have a similar distribution curve. This means that *typically* 80% of your results may actually come from only 20% of your efforts! Pareto's law can be seen in many situations – not literally 80/20 but certainly the principle that the majority of your results will often come from the minority of your efforts. http://www.allaboutagile.com/agile-principle-8-enough-is-enough/
Parking Lot Charts	Parking Lot Charts summarize the top-level project status. A parking-lot chart contains a large rectangular box for each **theme** (or grouping of user stories) in a release. Each box is annotated with the name of the theme, the number of stories in that theme, the number of story points or ideal days for those stories, and the percentage of the story points that are complete. http://www.change-vision.com/en/visualizingagileprojects.pdf
Payback Period	The length of time required to recover the cost of an investment. http://www.investopedia.com/terms/p/paybackperiod.asp
Personas	A persona, first introduced by Alan Cooper, defines an archetypical user of a system, an example of the kind of person who would interact with it. The idea is that if you want to design effective software, then it needs to be designed for a specific person. For the bank, potential personas for a customer could be named Frances Miller and Ross Williams. In other words, personas represent fictitious people which are based on your knowledge of real users (EXAM TIP: Specific exam question on why use "extreme" personas) http://www.agilemodeling.com/artifacts/personas.htm
Planning Poker	The idea behind Planning Poker is simple. Individual stories are presented for estimation. After a period of discussion, each participant chooses from his own deck the numbered card that represents his estimate of how much work is involved in the story under discussion. All estimates are kept private until each participant has chosen a card. At that time, all estimates are revealed (the card is played) and discussion in differences between the estimates begins. The goal is to keep discussing until variance on the estimate only varies by 1. They highest final number is used for the product backlog. http://store.mountaingoatsoftware.com/pages/planning-poker-in-detail
Pre-mortem	Also called a Futurespective: The pre-mortem activity is great for preparing for an upcoming release or challenge. With a different perspective, the activity guides the participants to talk about all that could go wrong. Then the conversation switches to a mitigation and action plan. http://riskology.co/pre-mortem-technique/
Process Tailoring	You can decide to tailor up, or tailor down. This is up to each organization to decide based on its own business needs. You just need to state your approach in your guidelines and then follow it.. Always tailor up if you want to increase control on your project, simplify your planning/ tailoring process, and run projects with appropriate agility, efficiency, and discipline. http://www.enterpriseunifiedprocess.com/essays/softwareProcessImprovement.html
Product Roadmap	Product/Portfolio planning is a key activity for the Agile Product Manager, which usually consists

	of planning and management of existing product sets, and defining new products for the portfolio. Now, in order to define the portfolio, the product manager has to develop a **product roadmap** in collaboration with her stakeholders that consists of new upcoming products and existing product plan updates based on the their current status. The product roadmap thus enables identifying future release windows and drives planning for tactical development. http://www.agilejournal.com/articles/columns/column-articles/2650-product-road-mapping-using-agile-principles
Progressive Elaboration	Progressive elaboration is defined by The PMBOK® Guide as continuously improving and detailing a plan as more detailed and specific information and more accurate estimates become available as the project progresses, and thereby producing more accurate and complete plans that result from the successive iterations of the planning process. 1. Decide on a release timebox for the project. This may be one week, two weeks, one month. Whatever your team is comfortable with. 2. Look at the requirements on a high level and have the team decide approximately what you can release in each release cycle. Since this is a high level, approximate estimate, you don't need to be too detailed. It's just there to provide a rough idea about how the releases will develop. 3. At every iteration planning meeting, sit with the customer/product owner and decide what you are going to do in that iteration. At this stage, you can ask for more details, and the team can come up with a more accurate estimate based on the details that you now know. 4. At the end of the iteration, update the high level overview with any new information that you now have. 5. Repeat steps 3 and 4 for every iteration. https://projectmanagementessentials.wordpress.com/2010/04/07/progressive-elaboration-moving-from-the-unknown-to-the-known/
Refactoring	Refactoring (noun): a change made to the internal structure of software to make it easier to understand and cheaper to modify without changing its observable behavior. http://martinfowler.com/bliki/DefinitionOfRefactoring.html
Relative Prioritization and Ranking	You use planning, ranking, and priority to specify which work the team should complete first. If you rank user stories, tasks, bugs, and issues, all team members gain an understanding of the relative importance of the work that they must accomplish. Ranking and priority fields are used to build several reports. You rank and prioritize work items when you review the backlog for a product or iteration. http://www.processimpact.com/articles/prioritizing.html
Relative Sizing using Story Points	Your team collaboratively estimates each user story in story points. In his book "Agile Estimation and Planning," Mike Cohn defines story points this way: "Story points are a unit of measure for expressing the overall size of a user story, feature or other piece of work." Story points are relative values that do not translate directly into a specific number of hours. Instead, story points help a team quantify the general size of the user story. These relative estimates are less precise so that they require less effort to determine, and they hold up better over time. By estimating in story points, your team will provide the general size of the user stories now and develop the more detailed estimation of hours of work later, when team members are about to

	implement the user stories. https://www.excella.com/insights/sizing-agile-stories-with-the-relative-sizing-grid Mike Cohn. 2005. Agile Estimating and Planning. Prentice Hall PTR, Upper Saddle River, NJ, USA
Research Story	Sometimes programmers won't be able to estimate a story because they don't know enough about the technology required to implement the story. In this case, create a story to research that technology. An example of a research story is "Figure out how to estimate 'Send HTML' story". Programmers will often use a spike solution (see Spike Solutions) to research the technology, so these sorts of stories are often called spike stories. Programmers can usually estimate how long it will take to research a technology even if they don't know the technology in question. If they can't even estimate how long the research will take, timebox the story as you do with bug stories. I find that a day is plenty of time for most spike stories, and half a day is sufficient for most. http://jamesshore.com/Agile-Book/stories.html

Retrospectives	The meeting performed at the end of an iteration or Sprint in which the project team identifies opportunities for improvement in the next iteration, or in their Agile Process in its entirety.
	Approach
	1. Set the Stage
	  • Lay the groundwork for the session by reviewing the goal and agenda. Create an environment for participation by checking in and establishing working agreements.
	2. Gather Data
	  • Review objective and subjective information to create a shared picture. Bring in each person's perspective. When the group sees the iteration from many points of view, they'll have greater insight.
	3. Generate Insights
	  • Step back and look at the picture the team created. Use activities that help people think together to delve beneath the surface.
	4. Decide What to Do
	  • Prioritize the team's insights and choose a few improvements or experiments that will make a difference for the team.
	5. Close the Retrospective
	  • Summarize how the team will follow up on plans and commitments. Thank team members for their hard work. Conduct a little retrospective on the retrospective, so you can improve too.
	
	http://www.estherderby.com/tag/retrospectives
	Esther Derby and Diana Larsen. 2006. *Agile Retrospectives: Making Good Teams Great.* Pragmatic Bookshelf.

Return On Investment (ROI)	A performance measure used to evaluate the efficiency of an investment or to compare the efficiency of a number of different investments. To calculate ROI, the benefit (return) of an investment is divided by the cost of the investment; the result is expressed as a percentage or a ratio. If an investment does not have a positive ROI, or if there are other opportunities with a higher ROI, then the investment should be not be undertaken. The return on investment formula: $$ROI = \frac{(\text{Gain from Investment} - \text{Cost of Investment})}{\text{Cost of Investment}}$$ (EXAM TIP: The only finance question that I had was on one how the Product Manager manages

	ROI) http://www.investopedia.com/terms/r/returnoninvestment.asp
Risk Areas	Tom DeMarco and Tim Lister identified five core risk areas common to all projects in their book, Waltzing with Bears: • Intrinsic Schedule Flaw (estimates that are wrong and undoable from day one, often based on wishful thinking) • Specification Breakdown (failure to achieve stakeholder consensus on what to build) • Scope Creep (additional requirements that inflate the initially accepted set) • Personnel Loss • Productivity Variation (difference between assumed and actual performance) http://leadinganswers.typepad.com/leading_answers/2007/04/the_top_five_so.html Tom DeMarco and Timothy Lister. 2003. Waltzing with Bears: Managing Risk on Software Projects. Dorset House Publ. Co., Inc., New York, NY, USA
Risk Adjusted Backlog	Risk Adjusted Backlog focuses on where investment needs to be undertaken, based on risk. The normal risk assessment database process will provide a decreasing list of priorities from the risk calculation: Potential Consequence x Likelihood. It may be necessary to make decisions on which of these should be dealt with first within each of the risk bands. Ideally one would fund and rectify all high and significant risks within the current financial year. However, constraints on both funding and the time to prepare and complete work may cause this ideal to be delayed. https://refinem.com/essential-agile-processes-part-8-risk-adjusted-backlog/
Risk Based Spike	Spikes, another invention of XP are a special type of story used to drive out risk and uncertainty in a user story or other project facet. Spikes may be used for a number of reasons: 1. Spikes may be used for basic research to familiarize the team with a new technology of domain 2. The story may be too big to be estimated appropriately and the team may use a spike to analyze the implied behavior so they can split the story into estimable pieces. 3. The story may contain significant technical risk and the team may have to do some research or prototyping to gain confidence in a technological approach that will allow them to commit the user story to some future timebox. 4. The story may contain significant functional risk, in that although the intent of the story may be understood, it is not clear how the system needs to interact with the user to achieve the benefit implied. http://www.scaledagileframework.com/spikes/
Risk Burn Down Graphs	Risk Burndown graphs are very useful for seeing if the total project risk is increasing or decreasing over time. It allows stakeholders to see instantly if we are reducing project risk.

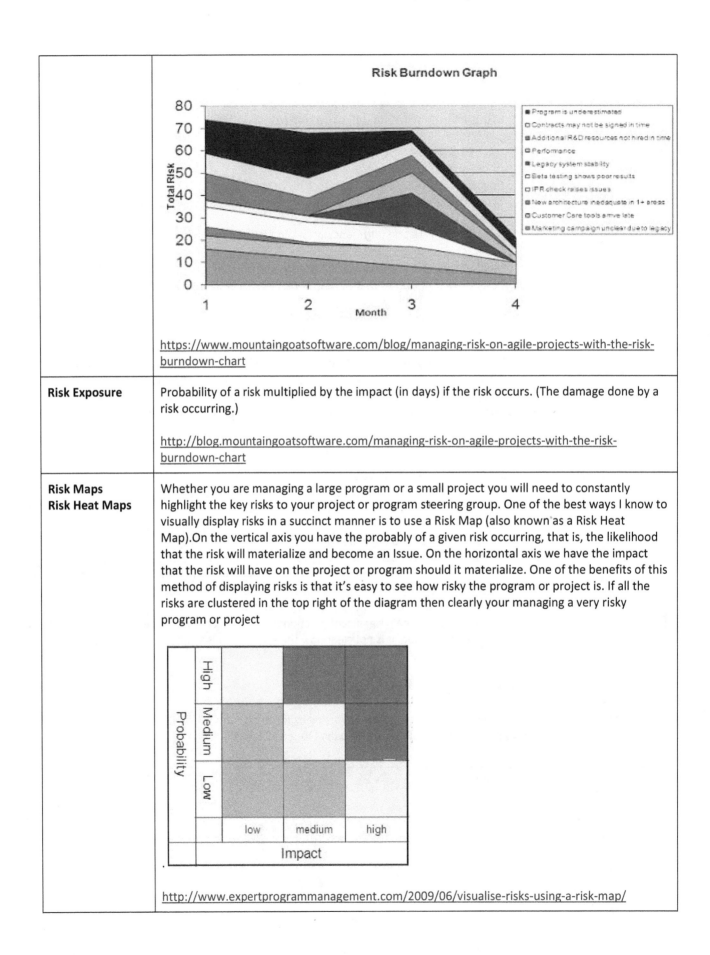

https://www.mountaingoatsoftware.com/blog/managing-risk-on-agile-projects-with-the-risk-burndown-chart

Risk Exposure	Probability of a risk multiplied by the impact (in days) if the risk occurs. (The damage done by a risk occurring.) http://blog.mountaingoatsoftware.com/managing-risk-on-agile-projects-with-the-risk-burndown-chart
Risk Maps **Risk Heat Maps**	Whether you are managing a large program or a small project you will need to constantly highlight the key risks to your project or program steering group. One of the best ways I know to visually display risks in a succinct manner is to use a Risk Map (also known as a Risk Heat Map).On the vertical axis you have the probably of a given risk occurring, that is, the likelihood that the risk will materialize and become an Issue. On the horizontal axis we have the impact that the risk will have on the project or program should it materialize. One of the benefits of this method of displaying risks is that it's easy to see how risky the program or project is. If all the risks are clustered in the top right of the diagram then clearly your managing a very risky program or project http://www.expertprogrammanagement.com/2009/06/visualise-risks-using-a-risk-map/

Risk Multipliers	Risk multipliers account for common risks, such as turnover, changing requirements, work disruption, and so forth. These risk multipliers allow you to set a date, estimate how many story points of work you'll get done, and be right. It's a simpler version of the risk curves you'll see in good books on estimating and project management. http://jamesshore.com/Blog/Use-Risk-Management-to-Make-Solid-Commitments.html
Scrum Ceremonies	There are four ceremonies • Sprint planning: the team meets with the product owner to choose a set of work to deliver during a sprint • Daily scrum: the team meets each day to share struggles and progress • Sprint reviews: the team demonstrates to the product owner what it has completed during the sprint • Sprint retrospectives: the team looks for ways to improve the product and the process (EXAM TIP: We did not go deeply into the Scrum Roles or Ceremonies in this Guide since this is the most commonly trained and well documented material. If you have not already attended a Scrum training, you should read Ken Schwaber's *Agile Project Management with Scrum*, or minimally, the latest Scrum guide: http://www.scrumguides.org
Servant Leadership	There are several differences between Traditional projects and true Agile projects that—from a project management perspective—can best be summed up by the concept of self organization. In traditional projects, the project manager not only provides the vision of the team, but also directs and manages the team on the more detailed daily tasks by maintaining an up to date project plan. This usually results in a leadership style perhaps best described as "command and control." Agile projects on the other hand, still include the concepts of planning, managing the work, and providing status, but these activities are addressed collectively by the team, because at the end of the day they are the ones most familiar with what actually needs to happen to accomplish the project's goals. In this case, the Project Leader is in more of a support and facilitation role, similar in concept to Robert Greenleaf's idea of the Servant Leader. As Mike Cohn puts it in his Certified Scrum Master Class, the Project Leader's primary responsibilities are to "move boulders and carry water"—in other words, remove obstacles that prevent the team from providing business value, and make sure the team has the environment they need to succeed. One model often used to describe the leadership style needed on agile projects is the Collaborative Leadership model suggested by Pollyanna Pixton: • Make sure you have the **right people** on the project team. The right people are defined as those individuals who have passion about the goal of the project, have the ability to do the project, and are provided with the proper capacity, or time to work on the project. • **Trust First**, rather than waiting for people to prove their trustworthiness. • **Let the team members propose the approach** to make the project a success. After all, they are the ones who best know how to do the work. • **Stand back** and let the team members do their work without hovering over them continuously asking for status or trying to direct their activities, and provide support along the way to make sure nothing gets in the way of their success http://www.projectconnections.com/articles/092806-mcdonald.html Pollyanna Pixton, Niel Nickolaisen, Todd Little, and Kent McDonald. 2009. Stand Back and Deliver: Accelerating Business Agility (1st ed.). Addison-Wesley Professional
Shu Ha Ri	Shu-Ha-Ri is a way of thinking about how you learn a technique. The name comes from Japanese martial arts (particularly Aikido), and Alistair Cockburn introduced it as a way of thinking about learning techniques and methodologies for software development.

	The idea is that a person passes through three stages of gaining knowledge: • **Shu:** In this beginning stage the student follows the teachings of one master precisely. He concentrates on how to do the task, without worrying too much about the underlying theory. If there are multiple variations on how to do the task, he concentrates on just the one way his master teaches him. • **Ha:** At this point the student begins to branch out. With the basic practices working he now starts to learn the underlying principles and theory behind the technique. He also starts learning from other masters and integrates that learning into his practice. • **Ri:** Now the student isn't learning from other people, but from his own practice. He creates his own approaches and adapts what he's learned to his own particular circumstances. • http://martinfowler.com/bliki/ShuHaRi.html
Signal Card	English translation of the Japanese word, Kanban
Spike Solutions	A spike solution, or spike, is a technical investigation. It's a small experiment to research the answer to a problem. For example, a programmer might not know whether Java throws an exception on arithmetic overflow. A quick ten-minute spike will answer the question. http://jamesshore.com/Agile-Book/spike_solutions.html
Sprint Review	At the end of each sprint a sprint review meeting is held. During this meeting the Scrum team shows what they accomplished during the sprint. Typically this takes the form of a demo of the new features. The sprint review meeting is intentionally kept very informal, typically with rules forbidding the use of PowerPoint slides and allowing no more than two hours of preparation time for the meeting. A sprint review meeting should not become a distraction or significant detour for the team; rather, it should be a natural result of the sprint. Participants in the sprint review typically include the Product Owner, the Scrum team, the ScrumMaster, management, customers, and developers from other projects. During the sprint review the project is assessed against the sprint goal determined during the Sprint planning meeting. Ideally the team has completed each product backlog item brought into the sprint, but it is more important that they achieve the overall goal of the Sprint. http://www.mountaingoatsoftware.com/scrum/sprint-review-meeting
Story Maps	User story mapping offers an alternative for traditional agile planning approaches like the Scrum product backlog. Instead of a simple list, stories are laid out as a two dimensional map. The map provides both a high level overview of the system under development and of the value it adds to the users (the horizontal axis), and a way to organize detailed stories into releases according to importance, priority, etc. (the vertical axis). The map shows how every user story fits in the full scope. Releases are defined by creating horizontal slices of user stories, each slice is a release. For the first release, it is recommended to build a minimal set of user stories covering all user goals, so that you build a minimal but complete system to validate functionality and architecture early. https://www.thoughtworks.com/insights/blog/story-mapping-visual-way-building-product-backlog
Sustainable Pace	To set your pace you need to take your iteration ends seriously. You want the most completed, tested, integrated, production ready software you can get each iteration. Incomplete or buggy software represents an unknown amount of future effort, so you can't measure it. If it looks like

	you will not be able to get everything finished by iteration end have an iteration planning meeting and re-scope the iteration to maximize your project velocity. Even if there is only one day left in the iteration it is better to get the entire team re-focused on a single completed task than many incomplete ones.
	Working overtime sucks the spirit and motivation out of your team. When your team becomes tired and demoralized they will get less work done, not more, no matter how many hours are worked. Becoming over worked today steals development progress from the future. You can't make realistic plans when your team does more work this month and less next month. Instead of pushing people to do more than humanly possible use a release planning meeting to change the project scope or timing.
	Fred Brooks made it clear that adding more people is also a bad idea when a project is already late. The contribution made by many new people is usually negative. Instead ramp up your development team slowly well in advance, as soon as you predict a release will be too late.
	A sustainable pace helps you plan your releases and iterations and keeps you from getting into a death march. Find your team's perfect velocity that will remain consistent for the entire project. Every team is different. Demanding this team increase velocity to match that team will actually lower their velocity long term. So whatever your team's velocity is just accept it, guard it, and use it to make realistic plans.
	http://www.extremeprogramming.org/rules/overtime.html
Tail Length	The tail is the time period from "code slush" (true code freezes are rare) or "feature freeze" to actual deployment. This is the time period when companies do some or all of the following: beta testing, regression testing, product integration, integration testing, documentation, defect fixing.
	http://www.allaboutagile.com/shortening-the-tail/
Task Boards	Similar to Kanban Boards, a task board tracks the progress of work that is part of an overall story.
	https://realtimeboard.com/blog/scrum-kanban-boards-differences/
Team Development Stages	**Tuckman's Group Development Model** **Forming** In the *first stages* of team building, the *forming* of the team takes place. The individual's behavior is driven by a desire to be accepted by the others, and avoid controversy or conflict. Serious issues and feelings are avoided, and people focus on being busy with routines, such as team organization, who does what, when to meet, etc. But individuals are also gathering information and impressions - about each other, and about the scope of the task and how to approach it. This is a comfortable stage to be in, but the avoidance of conflict and threat means that not much actually gets done. The team meets and learns about the opportunities and challenges, and then agrees on goals and begins to tackle the tasks. Team members tend to behave quite independently. They may be motivated but are usually relatively uninformed of the issues and objectives of the team. Team members are usually on their best behavior but very focused on themselves. Mature team members begin to model appropriate behavior even at this early phase. Sharing the knowledge of the concept of "Teams - Forming, Storming, Norming, Performing" is extremely helpful to the team. Supervisors of the team tend to need to be directive during this phase. The forming stage of any team is important because, in this stage, the members of the team get to know one another, exchange some personal information, and make new friends. This is also a good opportunity to see how each member of the team works as an individual and how they

	respond to pressure.
	Storming
	Every group will next enter the *storming* stage in which different ideas compete for consideration. The team addresses issues such as what problems they are really supposed to solve, how they will function independently and together and what leadership model they will accept. Team members open up to each other and confront each other's ideas and perspectives. In some cases *storming* can be resolved quickly. In others, the team never leaves this stage. The maturity of some team members usually determines whether the team will ever move out of this stage. Some team members will focus on minutiae to evade real issues.
	The *storming* stage is necessary to the growth of the team. It can be contentious, unpleasant and even painful to members of the team who are averse to conflict. Tolerance of each team member and their differences should be emphasized. Without tolerance and patience the team will fail. This phase can become destructive to the team and will lower motivation if allowed to get out of control. Some teams will never develop past this stage.
	Supervisors of the team during this phase may be more accessible, but tend to remain directive in their guidance of decision-making and professional behavior. The team members will therefore resolve their differences and members will be able to participate with one another more comfortably. The ideal is that they will not feel that they are being judged, and will therefore share their opinions and views.
	Norming
	The team manages to have one goal and come to a mutual plan for the team at this stage. Some may have to give up their own ideas and agree with others in order to make the team function. In this stage, all team members take the responsibility and have the ambition to work for the success of the team's goals.
	Performing
	It is possible for some teams to reach the *performing* stage. These high-performing teams are able to function as a unit as they find ways to get the job done smoothly and effectively without inappropriate conflict or the need for external supervision. By this time, they are motivated and knowledgeable. The team members are now competent, autonomous and able to handle the decision-making process without supervision. Dissent is expected and allowed as long as it is channeled through means acceptable to the team.
	Supervisors of the team during this phase are almost always participative. The team will make most of the necessary decisions. Even the most high-performing teams will revert to earlier stages in certain circumstances. Many long-standing teams go through these cycles many times as they react to changing circumstances. For example, a change in leadership may cause the team to revert to *storming* as the new people challenge the existing norms and dynamics of the team.
	http://en.wikipedia.org/wiki/Tuckman's_stages_of_group_development
Team Space	William Pietri put together a list of rules for great development spaces. Amongst the well documented suggestions like putting the team together, room for daily standup, enough whiteboards and information radiators other suggestions included,
	• Get collaboration-friendly desks – William suggested this as one of the big pitfalls. He mentioned that many companies would like to foster collaboration but end up having furniture which is hostile to it.
	• Minimize distractions – The recommended rules to minimize distractions for the development stations include no phones, no email or IM, no off-topic conversation, less foot traffic and executives stay on mute.
	• Only direct contributors sit in the room – No chickens and certainly not the receptionist nor the sales people who would mostly be on the phone.

	• Pleasant space – Good lighting, decent air, plants, decorations and snacks. http://www.infoq.com/news/2010/02/agile-team-spaces
Technical Debt Management	It's all "those *internal* things that you choose not to do now, but which will impede future development if left undone" [Ward Cunningham]. On the surface the application looks to be of high quality and in good condition, but these problems are hidden underneath. QA may even tell you that the application has quality and few defects, but there is still debt. If this debt isn't managed and reduced, the cost of writing/maintaining the code will eventually outweigh its value to customers. In addition, it has a real financial cost: The time developers spend dealing with the technical debt and the resulting problems takes away from the time they can spend doing work that's valuable to the organization. The hard-to-read code that underlies technical debt also makes it more difficult to find bugs. Again, the time lost trying to understand the code is time lost from doing something more valuable. http://www.infoq.com/articles/technical-debt-levison **Managing technical debt** • **Starting captured debt.** Even if it is just by encouraging developers to note issues as they are writing code in the comments of that code, or putting in place more formal peer review processes where debt is captured it is important to document debt as it accumulates. • **Start measuring debt**. Once captured, placing a value / cost to the debt created enables objective discussions to be made. It also enables reporting to provide the organization with transparency of their growing debt. I believe that this approach would enable application and product end of life discussions to be made earlier and with more accuracy. • **Adopt standard architectures and open source models.** The more people that look at a piece of code the more likely debt will be reduced. The simple truth of many people using the same software makes it simpler and less prone to debt. http://theagileexecutive.com/2010/09/01/forrester-on-managing-technical-debt/
Test First Development	Test-First programming involves producing automated unit tests for production code, before you write that production code. Instead of writing tests afterward (or, more typically, not ever writing those tests), you always begin with a unit test. For every small chunk of functionality in production code, you first build and run a small (ideally very small), focused test that specifies and validates what the code will do. This test might not even compile, at first, because not all of the classes and methods it requires may exist. Nevertheless, it functions as a kind of executable specification. You then get it to compile with minimal production code, so that you can run it and watch it fail. (Sometimes you expect it to fail, and it passes, which is useful information.) You then produce exactly as much code as will enable that test to pass. http://www.versionone.com/Agile101/Test-First_Programming.asp
Test-Driven Development	Test-Driven Development (TDD) is a special case of test-first programming that adds the element of continuous design. With TDD, the system design is not constrained by a paper design document. Instead you allow the process of writing tests and production code to steer the design as you go. Every few minutes, you refactor to simplify and clarify. If you can easily imagine a clearer, cleaner method, class, or entire object model, you refactor in that direction, protected the entire time by a solid suite of unit tests. The presumption behind TDD is that you

	cannot really tell what design will serve you best until you have your arms elbow-deep in the code. As you learn about what actually works and what does not, you are in the best possible position to apply those insights, while they are still fresh in your mind. And all of this activity is protected by your suites of automated unit tests.
	You might begin with a fair amount of up front design, though it is more typical to start with fairly modest design; some white-board UML sketches often suffice in the Extreme Programming world. But how much design you start with matters less, with TDD, than how much you allow that design to diverge from its starting point as you go. You might not make sweeping architectural changes, but you might refactor the object model to a large extent, if that seems like the wisest thing to do. Some shops have more political latitude to implement true TDD than others.
	http://www.versionone.com/Agile101/Test-First_Programming.asp
Throughput	Throughput is the amount of work items delivered in a given period of time (e.g. week, month, quarter).
	http://old.berriprocess.com/en/todas-las-categorias/item/62-analiticas-lean-kanban-rendimiento
Timeboxing	Timeboxing is a planning technique common in planning projects (typically for software development), where the schedule is divided into a number of separate time periods (timeboxes, normally two to six weeks long), with each part having its own deliverables, deadline and budget. Timeboxing is a core aspect of rapid application development (RAD) software development processes such as dynamic systems development method (DSDM) and agile software development.
	Scrum Timeboxes:
	• Sprint Planning – 2 sessions, 1 hour per week of sprint • Sprint Duration – 1-4 weeks • Daily Scrums – 15 mins/day • Sprint Review – 1 hours per week of sprint, 1 hour prep • Sprint Retrospective – 3 hours per sprint
	https://daymoframework.wordpress.com/2010/08/21/a-crash-course-in-time-boxing/
Trade-Off Matrix	Balancing the four constraints – compliance, cost, schedule, and scope – is not a trivial task. However, just like the Agile Triangle, the Tradeoff Matrix used in Agile software development applies to IT. In its software development variant, the Tradeoff matrix is an effective tool to decide between conflicting constraints, as follows:

	Fixed	Flexible	Accept
Scope			X
Schedule	X		
Cost		X	

Rules:

- *Fixed* trumps *Flexible* trumps *Accepts*
- Each column can contain only one check mark
- Two check marks can't have the same priority

Note: The specific check marks in Table 1 are merely illustrative. Any three check marks that adhere to the rules above are legitimate. In fact, the three check marks represent the organization's policy decision as to what really matters.

http://theagileexecutive.com/tag/tradeoff-matrix/

Transition Indicator	A transition indicator is a notification that a risk (i.e., something that will have a negative impact on the cost/schedule of the project *if* it occurs) has materialized and is in need of attention. http://www.informit.com/articles/article.aspx?p=2123314&seqNum=3
Usability Testing	Usability testing is a long-established, empirical and exploratory technique to answer questions such as "how would an end user respond to our software under realistic conditions?" It consists of observing a representative end user interacting with the product, given a goal to reach but no specific instructions for using the product. (For instance, a goal for usability testing of a furniture retailer's Web site might be "You've just moved and need to do something about your two boxes of books; use the site to find a solution.") http://guide.agilealliance.org/guide/usability.html
Use Cases	Use cases are sometimes used in heavyweight, control-oriented processes much like traditional requirements. The system is specified to a high level of completion via the use cases and then locked down with change control on the assumption that the use cases capture everything. Use cases attempt to bridge the problem of requirements not being tied to user interaction. A use case is written as a series of interactions between the user and the system, similar to a call and response where the focus is on how the user will use the system. In many ways, use cases are better than a traditional requirement because they emphasize user-oriented context. The value of the use case to the user can be divined, and tests based on the system response can be figured out based on the interactions. Use cases usually have two main components: Use case

	diagrams, which graphically describe actors and their use cases, and the text of the use case itself. http://en.wikipedia.org/wiki/Use_case
User Stories	A good way to think about a user story is that it is a reminder to have a conversation with your customer (in XP, project stakeholders are called customers), which is another way to say it's a reminder to do some just-in-time analysis. In short, user stories are very slim and high-level requirements artifacts. User stories are one of the primary development artifacts for Scrum and Extreme Programming (XP) project teams. A user story is a very high-level definition of a requirement, containing just enough information so that the developers can produce a reasonable estimate of the effort to implement it. http://www.agilemodeling.com/artifacts/userStory.htm
Value Stream Mapping	Value Stream Maps exist for two purposes: to help organizations identify and end wasteful activities. Finding problems and creating a more efficient process isn't easy; even the best organization can be made more efficient and effective. But bringing about substantive organizational change that actually eliminates waste is a tall order. It's comparatively easy to identify waste, but it's another matter entirely to stop waste from happening in the first place. Value Stream Maps can both sharpen an organization's skills in identifying waste and help drive needed change. But first things first: What a Value Stream Map is and how one can be intelligently produced. The examples and concepts that follow are based on applying a Value Stream Map to a software engineering organization, but these concepts are applicable to a wide range of settings. Value Stream Maps help us bring about organizational improvement, progress in our processes and methods, and most importantly, better software. Value Stream Maps can help both identify and stop waste in an organization http://www.ibm.com/developerworks/rational/library/10/howandwhytocreatevaluestreammapsforswengineerprojects/index.html?ca=drs-
Velocity	Velocity is an extremely simple, powerful method for accurately measuring the rate at which teams consistently deliver business value. To calculate velocity, simply add up the estimates of the features (user stories, requirements, backlog items, etc.) successfully delivered in an iteration. There are some simple guidelines for estimating initial velocity prior to completing the first iteration but after that point teams should use proven, historical measures for planning features. Within a short time, velocity typically stabilizes and provides a tremendous basis for improving the accuracy and reliability of both near-term and longer-term project planning. Agile delivery cycles are very small so velocity emerges and can be validated very early in a project and then relied upon to improve project predictability. http://www.versionone.com/agile-101/agile-scrum-velocity/
Wide Band Delphi	Estimation method is a consensus-based technique for estimating effort 1. Coordinator presents each expert with a specification and an estimation form. 2. Coordinator calls a group meeting in which the experts discuss estimation issues with the coordinator and each other. 3. Experts fill out forms anonymously. 4. Coordinator prepares and distributes a summary of the estimates 5. Coordinator calls a group meeting, specifically focusing on having the experts discuss

	points where their estimates vary widely 6. Experts fill out forms, again anonymously, and steps 4 to 6 are iterated for as many rounds as appropriate. http://en.wikipedia.org/wiki/Wideband_delphi
WIP Limits	Limiting work in process (WIP) to match your team's development capacity helps ensure the traffic density does not increase the capacity of your team. The Kanban board will help you get to the right WIP limit as you become better at it. Without WIP limits you will continue to pile up partially completed work in the pipe thereby creating the phantom traffic jam. Adding to your WIP without completing anything just increases the duration of all tasks in the queue. If you are a product development shop, having a large duration (lead time) can significantly affect your company's profitability. http://www.kanbanway.com/importance-of-kanban-work-in-progress-wip-limits
Wireframes	A wireframe is a "low fidelity" prototype. This non-graphical artifact shows the skeleton of a screen, representing its structure and basic layout. It contains and localizes contents, features, navigation tools and interactions available to the user. The wireframe is usually: • black and white, • accompanied by some annotations to describe the behavior of the elements (default or expected states, error cases, values, content source…), their relationships and their importance, • often put in context within a storyboard (a sequence of screens in a key scenario) • refined again and again • used as a communication tool serving as an element of conversation and confirmation of "agile" user stories http://www.agile-ux.com/tag/wireframe/
Agile Roles	
Scrum Roles	(EXAM TIP: I did not go deeply into the Scrum Roles or Ceremonies since this is the most commonly trained material. If you have not already attended a Scrum training, you should read Ken Schwaber's *Agile Project Management with Scrum,* or minimally, read the latest Scrum guide by him and Jeff Sutherland: http://www.scrumguides.org
Product Owner	The **product owner** decides what will be built and in which order. • Defines the features of the product or desired outcomes of the project • Chooses release date and content • Ensures profitability (ROI) • Prioritizes features/outcomes according to market value • Adjusts features/outcomes and priority as needed • Accepts or rejects work results • Facilitates scrum planning ceremony

	http://www.scrumguides.org
Scrum Master	The ScrumMaster is a facilitative team leader who ensures that the team adheres to its chosen process and removes blocking issues. • Ensures that the team is fully functional and productive • Enables close cooperation across all roles and functions • Removes barriers • Shields the team from external interferences • Ensures that the process is followed, including issuing invitations to daily scrums, sprint reviews, and sprint planning • Facilitates the daily scrums http://www.scrumguides.org
Team	• Is cross-functional • Is right-sized (the ideal size is seven -- plus/minus two -- members) • Selects the sprint goal and specifies work results • Has the right to do everything within the boundaries of the project guidelines to reach the sprint goal • Organizes itself and its work • Demos work results to the product owner and any other interested parties. http://www.scrumguides.org
Extreme Programming (XP) Roles	
XP Coach	The XP Coach role helps a team stay on process and helps the team to learn. A coach brings an outside perspective to help a team see themselves more clearly. The coach will help balance the needs of delivering the project while improving the use of the practices. A coach or team of coaches supports the Customer Team, the Developer Team, and the Organization. The decisions that coaches make should always stem from the XP values (communication, simplicity, feedback, and courage) and usually move toward the XP practices. As such, familiarity with the values and practices is a prerequisite. The coach must command the respect required to lead the respective teams. The coach must possess people skills and be effective in influencing the actions of the teams. http://epf.eclipse.org/wikis/xp/xp/roles/xp_coach_60023190.html
XP Customer	The XP Customer role has the responsibility of defining what is the right product to build, determining the order in which features will be built and making sure the product actually works. The XP Customer writes system features in the form of user stories that have business value. Using the planning game, he chooses the order in which the stories will be done by the development team. He also defines acceptance tests that will be run against the system to prove that the system is reliable and does what is required. The customer prioritizes user stories, the team estimates them. http://epf.eclipse.org/wikis/xp/xp/roles/xp_customer_6D7CB91B.html

XP Programmer	The XP Programmer is responsible for implementing the code to support the user stories http://epf.eclipse.org/wikis/xp/xp/roles/xp_programmer_D005E927.html-
XP Programmer (Administrator)	The XP Programmer (Administrator) role includes most of the traditional software development technical roles, such as designer, implementer, integrator, and administrator. In the administrator role, the programmer deals with establishing the physical working environment http://epf.eclipse.org/wikis/xp/xp/roles/xp_system_administrator_92735060.html
XP Tracker	The three basic things the XP Tracker will track are the release plan (user stories), the iteration plan (tasks) and the acceptance tests. The tracker can also keep track of other metrics, which may help in solving problems the team is having. A good XP Tracker has the ability to collect the information without disturbing the process significantly. http://epf.eclipse.org/wikis/xp/xp/roles/xp_tracker_AD8A6C9F.html
XP Tester	The primary responsibility of the XP Tester is to help the customer define and implement acceptance tests for user stories. The XP Tester is also responsible for running the tests frequently and posting the results for the whole team to see. As the number of tests grow, the XP Tester will likely need to create and maintain some kind of tool to make it easier to define them, run them, and gather the results quickly. Whereas knowledge of the applications target domain is provided by the customer, the XP Tester needs to support the customer by providing: • Knowledge of typical software failure conditions and the test techniques that can be employed to uncover those errors. • Knowledge of different techniques to implement and run tests, including understanding of and experience with test automation http://epf.eclipse.org/wikis/xp/xp/roles/xp_tester_44877D41.html

The Agile Manifesto

In February 2001, 17 software developers met at the Snowbird, Utah resort, to discuss lightweight development methods. They published the *Manifesto for Agile Software Development* to define the approach now known as agile software development. Some of the manifesto's authors formed the Agile Alliance, a nonprofit organization that promotes software development according to the manifesto's principles.

The Agile Manifesto reads, in its entirety, as follows:

We are uncovering better ways of developing software by doing it and helping others do it. Through this work we have come to value:

Individuals and interactions over processes and tools

Working software over comprehensive documentation

Customer collaboration over contract negotiation

Responding to change over following a plan

That is, while there is value in the items on the right, we value the items on the left more.

The meanings of the manifesto items on the left within the agile software development context are described below:

• Individuals and Interactions – in agile development, self-organization and motivation are important, as are interactions like co-location and pair programming.
• Working software – working software will be more useful and welcome than just presenting documents to

clients in meetings.

- Customer collaboration – requirements cannot be fully collected at the beginning of the software development cycle, therefore continuous customer or stakeholder involvement is very important.
- Responding to change – agile development is focused on quick responses to change and continuous development.

Twelve principles underlie the Agile Manifesto, including:

1. Our highest priority is to satisfy the customer through early and continuous delivery of valuable software.
2. Welcome changing requirements, even late in development. Agile processes harness change for the customer's competitive advantage.
3. Deliver working software frequently, from a couple of weeks to a couple of months, with a preference to the shorter timescale.
4. Business people and developers must work together daily throughout the project.
5. Build projects around motivated individuals. Give them the environment and support they need, and trust them to get the job done.
6. The most efficient and effective method of conveying information to and within a development team is face-to-face conversation.
7. Working software is the primary measure of progress.
8. Agile processes promote sustainable development. The sponsors, developers, and users should be able to maintain a constant pace indefinitely.
9. Continuous attention to technical excellence and good design enhances agility.
10. Simplicity--the art of maximizing the amount of work not done--is essential.
11. The best architectures, requirements, and designs emerge from self-organizing teams.
12. At regular intervals, the team reflects on how to become more effective, then tunes and adjusts its behavior accordingly.

http://agilemanifesto.org/